Most immediately this means that Mosca and Volpone put all
their minds and energies into bilking the fools and enjoying those
pleasures of the senses and the mind which fortune calls them to.
But the particular form their cunning takes is of central importance in the play. They are above all else master actors; not the
kind of actors who learn their lines beforehand and move according to a pre-established plot, but improvisers like the *commedia
dell' arte* players—referred to in the text in several places—who
extemporize their lines and action and make up their plot as they
go along. Volpone is an unusually impressive actor. He plays a
sick and dying man to perfection, coughing at the right moment,
seeming to recover slightly when necessary, moving his hands
weakly or lying perfectly immobile as the situation requires.
When stirred by lust for Celia, he typically solves the problem of
how to see her by assuming another disguise, of mountebank,
which he plays so well that the mountebank himself could not
have been sure, as Mosca tells him, that he was an impostor. After
Bonario interrupts his attempted rape of Celia, Volpone is called
on to play his most difficult part, an absolutely impotent and
dying old man. Despite the stringent requirements of the role—
that he lie absolutely still and *look* as if he were on the verge of
death—he delivers a magnificent performance. Mosca, with all
the professional perfectionism of a Stanislavsky, accuses him of
sweating while he lay there; but it is nevertheless an excellent
piece of work. And finally, in order to torment even more the
fortune hunters who already have been cheated of their money,
Volpone puts on the costume of a sergeant of the court and plays
an excellent clown, an ironic Dogberry.

But as excellent an actor as Volpone is, he is surpassed by
Mosca, who can, he exults, "change a visor swifter than a
thought." His great dramatic forte is flexibility. Where Volpone
once having assumed a role continues to play it without much
change, Mosca shifts roles from moment to moment. He can in

swift succession be the humble servant of the legacy hunters, the crying friend of virtue who advises Bonario that his father is about to disinherit him, the smiling pander, the modest but stern inheritor of Volpone's fortune, the impressive and sober *magnifico*. There seems no end to his resources, and all that he plays he plays superbly. He is what he chooses to be. But even beyond the range of his acting, we must not forget that with such rare exceptions as the soliloquy at the beginning of Act III, he is playing two roles simultaneously: to Volpone he plays the subtle and obsequious servant; to the fools he plays whatever the occasion requires him to be; but underneath he remains the clever opportunist simply waiting for a chance to bilk his master.

Mosca has other theatrical talents as well. He is an excellent make-up man who carefully anoints Volpone's eyes to appear like those of a dying man; and he sees to it that they are kept sufficiently dulled. As costumer he arranges Volpone's fur robes on the "sick" man, and later finds the uniform of a sergeant for him. As producer he oversees the erection of the mountebank's platform stage in Act II. As a director he truly excels. In the first four acts of the play, Mosca arranges the scenes of all the little plays within the play. In the sick-room play of Acts I and III he prepares Volpone for his role, directs him when to enter the bed, coaches him on how to act, and then opens and closes the curtains of Volpone's bed-stage at the proper moments.

His masterwork is, however, the court-room play of Act IV. Here he takes a variety of actors of widely differing capabilities and interests—Volpone, Voltore, Corbaccio, Corvino, and Lady Wouldbe—and creates a smoothly working ensemble. First, he passes among them, distributing their parts, i.e. making sure they know the lies they will tell. The lead is assigned to Voltore the lawyer, who is, as befits his profession, a considerable actor, able to speak

To every cause, and things mere contraries,
Till . . . hoarse again, yet all be law;
That, with most quick agility, could turn,
And re-turn; make knots, and undo them . . .

(I.3.54–57)

After Voltore struts about and delivers his rather old-fashioned speech, accompanied by elaborate gestures, the witnesses are smoothly introduced to play their stock parts: Corbaccio, the kind old father cruelly treated by his son; Corvino, the gentle, forgiving husband taken advantage of by his lewd wife; Lady Wouldbe, an innocent, outraged wife. When Corbaccio or Corvino have doubts or hesitate, Mosca is there to prompt and reassure them. At just the right moment the apparently dying Volpone is carried into court. So well-designed and smooth-running is Mosca's theatrical machinery that the innocents Bonario and Celia, despite their own efforts to state the truth, are drawn into Mosca's plot and designated the villains of the piece.

It is no wonder that Mosca considers this his "masterwork," and Volpone is forced to agree that Mosca has "played [the] prize" (V.2.15). But Volpone is not content to let the deceptions rest here, and he insists on directing two more plays himself, both of which lead to disaster. The first is the scene in which he retires, as director and audience, behind a "traverse" curtain while Mosca pretends to be the heir to the fortune and drives away each of the fortune hunters in turn. The second is his pretense of being a sergeant. Both plays, while amusing for Volpone, are failures by the theatrical standards set up within the larger play. All of Mosca's plays present the fools with flattering images of themselves, persuade them that they are handsome, generous, noble, dignified, and, above all, full of promise for the future. The results are most gratifying: gold, plate, and jewels find their way into Mosca's hand and Volpone's treasure chest. So long as Mosca directs, illusions remain unshattered; but Volpone has a

9

savage, satiric streak in him, and the two plays he arranges in Act V expose the inheritance seekers for the arrant fools and corrupt beings they essentially are. The result is disaster for Volpone's plans. The fools strike back in revenge, and all is at last uncovered.

As *Volpone* proceeds, the acting theme is strengthened by the knaves' constant use of the language of the theater: plot, forced posture, epilogue, scene, feign, mask, zany, action, Pantalone; we begin to have the odd feeling that we are watching a play within a play or—as the levels of deception multiply—a play within a play within a play. At times the theatrical quality present in language and action is fully realized on stage, and we are presented openly with a theater within a theater. The grotesque interlude presented by Nano and Androgyno in Act I, Scene 2, and the performance of Volpone as mountebank on the platform stage erected on the real stage are clear-cut instances, like "The Murder of Gonzago" in *Hamlet*, of smaller performances within the larger. But Volpone's huge bed with its movable curtains and acting space on which he plays out his sickness is also a small stage—an "inner stage"—and in Act V, Scene 2, Volpone and Mosca, using a traverse, construct a second theater in which Mosca plays out the comedy of driving each of the fortune hunters out of his humor, stripping him of his hopes and of his pretenses. The court room with its performers and its spectators also reproduces the physical arrangements of the theater.

Just as the theatrical metaphor which is woven into every scene becomes manifest in a number of small theaters within the real theater, so does the idea of acting. Volpone and Mosca are nearly always acting, but from time to time they retire to the wings, where, like the professionals they are, they discuss the fine points of their art and congratulate each other on their performances. Mosca, as I have mentioned, can be hypercritical and refer maliciously to the fact that Volpone broke out with sweat under the strain of acting a dying man in court, but at other times he can generously praise a fine performance. After Voltore has twisted truth to falsehood in court with a ringing voice, fine gestures ("action"), and beautiful pacing, Mosca can exclaim admiringly, "I'd have your tongue, sir, tipped with gold for this." When Volpone after his masterful impersonation of the mountebank Scoto worries that his make-up may not have been sufficient ("Is not the color of my beard and eyebrows to make me known?"), Mosca assures him that "Scoto himself could hardly have distinguished." Volpone then smugly exclaims, "I did it well." Volpone, equally appreciative of Mosca's abilities, is always bursting with admiration and praise for the particularly skillful ways in which Mosca acts his parts for the fortune hunters.

The idea of "playing" is the central theme of *Volpone*, and ultimately all the other details of the intricately wrought play feed into this master image. Gold, for example, which is so prominent throughout, is finally but one of the many masquerades. Its worshippers make of it a god, the sun, learning, honor, virtue; but it is finally no more than dull, heavy, and spiritless metal—dross—disguised to resemble the truly good. The classical references which Jonson works into his text frequently refer to some instance of "acting": Jacob covered with goatskins pretending to be Esau to cheat his brother of his blessing, Jove disguised as a shower of gold in order to enjoy Danaë, Lollia Paulina covered with jewels to look like starlight.

Obviously the iteration of this theme reveals that a world and men given over entirely to materialism are unreal, mere pretenses. But this is almost a moral commonplace, and Jonson's anatomizing knife cuts deeper. Volpone and Mosca, and to a lesser degree Voltore and the other fools, think of man as *homo ludens* and his genius as *ludere*, to act, to play. Where for a fool like Voltore this means no more than pretending to be the honest advocate for the cause that pays the best, for a Volpone and a

Mosca playing becomes the exercise of a godlike power. Playing the roles of dying men and humble parasite are for them only rehearsals for metamorphosis, complete transcendence of reality. Volpone's belief in the powers of acting appears most clearly in his sensuous and passionate temptation of Celia, one of the best-known speeches in Renaissance drama. His imagination runs riot as he pictures for her the incredible wealth they will enjoy and the sensual pleasures they will share, if only she will submit to him. All the world will be plundered to supply them with a moment's delight, a jewel, a rare dish, a luxurious bath; and then they will pass on to the greatest of pleasures, love:

> my dwarf shall dance,
> My eunuch sing, my fool make up the antic.
> Whilst we, in changèd shapes, act Ovid's tales,
> Thou like Europa now, and I like Jove,
> Then I like Mars, and thou like Erycine;
> So of the rest, till we have quite run through,
> And wearied all the fables of the gods.
> Then will I have thee in more modern forms,
> Attirèd like some sprightly dame of France,
> Brave Tuscan lady, or proud Spanish beauty . . .
>
> (III.7.219–28)

His appetite for infinite variety and his fertile imagination hurry him onward to describe even more shapes which she will assume to avoid satiety: Persian, Turk, courtesan, "quick negro," "cold Russian"; and he will "meet" her,

> in as many shapes;
> Where we may, so, transfuse our wand'ring souls
> Out at our lips, and score up sums of pleasures,
> That the curious shall not know
> How to tell them as they flow . . .

The action discernible in these lines is the action of human genius as Volpone understands it: to "flow" by means of acting, to change shapes from mere man to the immortal gods—Jove, Mars, Erycine—and thus enjoy endless pleasures and endless change.

Mosca is not so flamboyant as Volpone, but the achievements of his acting put Volpone to shame:

> Success hath made me wanton. I could skip
> Out of my skin, now, like a subtle snake,
> I am so limber.
>
> (III.1.5–7)

But as he warms to the praise of his own acting, the ability to skip out of his skin becomes a minor accomplishment, for he feels that he (23–29):

> can rise
> And stoop, almost together, like an arrow;
> Shoot through the air as nimbly as a star;
> Turn short as doth a swallow; and be here,
> And there, and here, and yonder, all at once;
> Present to any humor, all occasion;
> And change a visor swifter than a thought . . .

Here is man altogether freed by his ability to act from the limitations reality imposes on ordinary men! Not only can he be anything he wishes, he can be several persons in several places at once!

Acting is for Volpone and Mosca a magical power, a short cut to fulfillment of boundless desire which avoids such unpleasant realities as old age, decay, satiation, poverty. Acting opens up for them a brave new world of the imagination where man can contend with the gods themselves, as Volpone boasts to Celia: "In varying figures I would have contended / With the blue Proteus . . ." (III.7.152–53). If their adoration of gold suggests Volpone's and Mosca's materialism, their faith in acting marks them as believers in the theory that man can make of himself whatever he wills to be, even a god. They are thus the spokesmen for progress, the kind of progress based on increase of material possessions and rugged individualism. And in this they are one with such titans as Tamburlaine, Faustus, Richard III, Edmund, Lady Macbeth, and Milton's Satan, who all express—before coming to tragic awareness—the optimistic Renaissance view:

> The mind is its own place, and in it self
> Can make a Heav'n of Hell, a Hell of Heav'n.
>
> *(Paradise Lost,* I.254–55)

We cannot help being moved by the power of such a belief, and a comic figure such as Volpone, as well as a defiant Satan thundering from the depths of hell, has a magnificence about him, a gusto for experience and a turbulent vitality that is attractive. To understand, however, the full grandeur which this attitude toward man and his possibilities is capable of reaching, we must look at a passage in the *Oration on the Dignity of Man* written by Pico della Mirandola in 1486, where transformation, i.e. acting, is argued very seriously as the source of human greatness. Pico is describing creation. God, he says,

took man as a creature of indeterminate nature, and assigning him a place in the middle of the world, addressed him thus: "Neither a fixed abode, nor a form that is thine alone, nor any function peculiar to thyself have we given thee, Adam, to the end that according to thy longing and according to thy judgment thou mayest have and possess what abode, what form, and what functions thou thyself shalt desire. The nature of all other beings is limited and constrained within the bounds of laws prescribed by Us. Thou, constrained by no limits, in accordance with thine own free will, in whose hand we have placed thee, shalt ordain for thyself the limits of thy nature. We have set thee at the world's center that thou mayest from thence more easily observe whatever is in the world. We have made thee neither of heaven nor of earth, neither mortal nor immortal, so that with freedom of choice and with honor, as though the maker and molder of thyself in whatever shape thou shalt prefer. Thou shalt have the power to degenerate into the lower forms of life, which are brutish. Thou shalt have the power, out of thy soul's judgment, to be reborn into the higher forms, which are divine . . ." Who would not admire this our chameleon? Or who could more greatly admire aught else whatever? It is man who Asclepius of Athens, arguing from his mutability of character and from his self-transforming nature, on just grounds says was symbolized by Proteus in the mysteries. Hence those metamorphoses renowned among the Hebrews and the Pythagoreans.[3]

The freedom of will which this passage celebrates so joyfully is, of course, orthodox Christian doctrine, but Pico gives man a great deal more freedom in choosing his own ends—"the maker and molder of thyself"—than had ever been allowed. And the Catholic Church condemned as heretical the theses which Pico proposed to argue in 1487 and for which the *Oration* was intended as a preface. This passage, though Pico would surely have objected, would have been acclaimed by Volpone and Mosca as an exact statement of their own beliefs in man's limitlessness; but Ben Jonson held more traditional views than either Pico or the characters in *Volpone*.

"For effective attack," Northrop Frye notes, the satirist "must reach some kind of impersonal level, and that commits the attacker, if only by implication, to a moral standard."[4] It is quite clear that a moral standard is present in *Volpone*, but the ethic is implicit rather than explicit. The play does not have a moral spokesman denouncing this world in the thundering terms of a Jeremiah, but action and speeches are constructed in a way which reveals the values that gold is obliterating. When Volpone in his opening speech substitutes gold for the sun, for religion, for family, for friends, and for society, we are reminded forcefully of the values and the moral principles which the sun and these traditional institutions embody. Irony is thus Jonson's chief satiric

---

3. Trans. E. L. Forbes, in *The Renaissance Philosophy of Man*, ed. Cassirer, Kristeller, and Randall (Chicago, 1948), pp. 224–26.

4. *Anatomy of Criticism* (Princeton, 1957), p. 225.

15

technique: the world of the play is an upside-down world, the mirror world that satirists so often create—in *The Dunciad, A Modest Proposal, Brave New World*—where everything is the reverse of what any good man, and even the not so good, knows it rightly should be.[5]

To understand the range and consistency of the irony in *Volpone* we shall have to look briefly at that physical and moral arrangement of the universe which E. M. W. Tillyard has called the Elizabethan World Picture, and which was in one form or another the central image of creation from the time of Aristotle until the eighteenth century. Under one of its alternative names, the Great Chain of Being, it is the organizing principle behind Milton's *Paradise Lost,* Pope's *Essay on Man*, and Swift's *Gulliver's Travels*, as well as Jonson's plays and many other works of the Renaissance. The Great Chain of Being is a way of ordering the multiplicity and variety of existence into a meaningful whole. The links in this chain, which binds all creation together, are the various levels or categories of being beginning with God at the top and moving downward through the angels, man, animals, and plants, to the lowest link, inanimate objects. Inanimate objects simply *are*, they occupy space; the plants *are* and can feed themselves and reproduce; animals do all this and in addition have senses, mobility, and memory. Man possesses all these faculties and adds to them understanding, i.e. reason, and will. The higher beings, angels in the Christian system, are pure understanding; while God is above them as pure being. The Great Chain is a ladder upward, with each category of life possessing

---

5. "What a rare punishment / Is avarice to itself" (I.4.142–43) Volpone comments on the ironic way Corbaccio's greed leads him to the loss of the very gold he so desperately seeks. Jonson's method is simply to expand the meaning of this conventional description of the nature of sin by allowing greed not only to defeat itself by its own efforts but to condemn itself from its own mouth.

in addition to all the faculties of the categories below some unique faculty which distinguishes it from its inferiors. Within each category the various kinds are hierarchically arranged in the same manner: among the animals the parasite has only mobility and the sense of touch and is therefore lower on the scale than the fox, who has all five senses plus memory.

Man is, of course, the link in the chain which most intrigued the philosophers, and the one which concerns us here. Most frequently he is spoken of as a microcosm, a little world, because he contained in himself all the faculties, though none pre-eminently, of the remainder of creation. He had the ability of the plants to grow and reproduce, the senses and mobility of the animals, and the reason of the angels. But he could not grow as mighty as the oak, he could not run with the speed of the antelope, nor was his reason as pure as that of the angels, who could apprehend God clearly and therefore obey him without question. Having all these faculties, man was, as Pico shows, a series of possibilities rather than an actuality, and since God in addition to endowing man with reason which enabled him to know right from wrong had also given him freedom of will, it followed that man was free to choose whether he would realize his angelic nature by exercising his reason or his animal nature by following the pull of his lower faculties: greed, the perversion of the nutritive faculties; lust, the perversion of the reproductive faculties; voluptuousness, the perversion of the sensory faculties. Pico in his "Oration" is, of course, working within the theory of the Great Chain, but he is wildly optimistic about the pleasure of free choice, the range of human possibility, and the inevitability of man choosing his angelic nature over his bestial. Certain other Renaissance thinkers, Machiavelli and John Calvin, for example, were equally pessimistic, believing as Calvin says, that "our nature is not only destitute of all good, but is so fertile in all evils that it cannot remain inactive . . . every thing in man, the understanding and

will, the soul and body, is polluted and engrossed by concupiscence."[6]

But there was in the Renaissance, as always, a middle way, a
balanced view of the possibility of man controlling the beast in
himself and nurturing his reason. Sir John Hayward expresses this
view (which would also seem to have been Jonson's) in terms
which are so appropriate for *Volpone* that I shall quote at some
length:

> Certainly of all the creatures under heaven, which have received
> being from God, none degenerate, none forsake their naturall dignitie
> and being, but onely man; Onely man, abandoning the dignitie of his
> proper nature, is changed like *Proteus,* into divers forms. And this is
> occasioned by reason of the libertie of his will: which is a facultie that
> transformeth men into so many things, as with violent appetite it doth
> pursue. Hence it proceeded, that in the creation of other things, God
> approved them, and saw that they were good; because hee gave them
> a stable and permanent nature. But of the goodnesse of man no men-
> tion at all. Mans goodnesse was left unapproved at the first because
> God gave him liberty of will; either to embrace vertue and bee like
> unto God, or to adhere to sensualitie and be like unto beasts.

> And as every kind of beast is principally inclined to one sensualitie
> more then to any other; so man transformeth himselfe into that beast,
> to whose sensualitie he principallie declines . . . This did the ancient
> wisemen shadow foorth by their fables of certaine persons changed
> into such beasts, whose crueltie, or sotterie, or other brutish nature
> they did express.[7]

Hayward describes perfectly what happens in *Volpone*. The
beast fable which underlies the play and the names of the characters—the fox, the crow, the vulture, the parrot, the flesh fly—
make it clear that the men who bear these names have been

---

6. *Institutes of the Christian Religion,* II.1.8.

7. *David's Tears* (London, 1623), pp. 251-52. The beginning of this
passage is quoted by Tillyard, *Elizabethan World Picture* (London, 1943),
p. 68.

transformed by their cunning and greed into the beasts to whose sensuality they "principally decline." The animal imagery—wolf, hyena, chameleon, crocodile, tortoise, swine, hog-louse—which appears throughout the play also serves to remind us that we are watching a spectacle of men turning into beasts. We might add that even as the characters become animals, they also become mere caricatures of living men, utter fools devoid of common sense, let alone reason, who can be persuaded to part with all their virtues and possessions in the fatuous hope of coming into great wealth. Mosca describes them in terms which reduce them below the level even of animal and fool to that of dirt, mere gross matter:

> Merchants may talk of trade, and your great signors
> Of land that yields well; but if Italy
> Have any glebe more fruitful than these fellows,
> I am deceived.

> (V.2.29–32)

All the characters of the play, with the exception of Celia and Bonario, move themselves downward on the scale of being. By choosing their lower faculties over their higher, they succeed in reducing themselves to animals and clods. But Jonson turns a simple moral point into the chief structural principle of his play by use of dramatic irony. Each of the gold seekers, from Volpone to Sir Politic, thinks of himself as rising in both the social and the hierarchical scale by his efforts. Voltore considers himself well on the way to being the richest and most learned advocate in Venice; Corbaccio thinks he will live forever like the angels; Lady Wouldbe with her painting and her chatter thinks she has made a great lady of herself; Sir Politic with his empty-headed schemes and his idle rumors feels that he has become a great statesman and a mercantile wizard. What they actually are is always grossly apparent to all but themselves, and the great joke, for Mosca and Volpone as well as the audience, is that purely by their own great efforts and expense have they made themselves into vultures, crows, and parrots.

The transformations of Volpone and Mosca are considerably more intricate and more interesting, and an examination of their degeneration reveals the extreme care with which Jonson constructed his play. Both of these master spirits of the play regard all the other characters as fools and potential sources of profit. But Volpone and Mosca are supremely unaware that they are victims of the same irony as their victims. Elevating the gold coin over the sun in the first lines of the play is, as I have said, Volpone's crucial act, and like all other actions in the play it is heavy with irony. What Volpone considers a raising, both of gold and of himself, is in fact a lowering. Gold, a heavy, drossy, inanimate metal has been placed above pure fire, a reversal of the proper order of the elements which in the Great Chain properly ascend in purity, and in the arrangement of the cosmos from water and earth through air to fire. And in choosing gold over the heat of the true sun, i.e. inert matter over vital spirit, Volpone is, by analogue, preferring the lower to the higher elements in the world and in himself. Therefore, what he regards as a supreme triumph, in fact symbolizes disaster for him as a man. Sir John Hayward again supplies an appropriate warning to man in terms which suggest the full meaning of "sun": "You are now in passage through a wide and wilde forrest; wherein you may be easily lost, wherein easily you may lose the use of that sunne, which should both enlighten and direct you to your journeys end."[8]

Volpone and Mosca believe their genius is most fully expressed in their ability to act, to play a part, to make of themselves what they will. Each "act" raises them higher in the scale of being, they believe, until in Volpone's case he becomes nothing less than

8. *David's Tears*, p. 255.

a god, Mars, Jove; while Mosca considers that he is able to transcend altogether the limitations of the flesh through a skill which enables him, like angels or other pure essences, "to be here, and there, and here, and yonder, all at once." But their progression is in fact a degeneration. In social terms this is immediately evident. Volpone begins as a *magnifico*, a noble of Venice occupying a place of dignity and responsibility in the state. In Act II he appears in the role of an itinerant mountebank, a mere quack living by his wits and without an accepted place in society. From this disguise he passes on to playing a clownish sergeant of the court, a minor hireling of the state subject to whipping. In the end he is reduced to the status of eternal prisoner confined in irons—but this is no role, it is the form which manifests finally and irrevocably the dangerous beast which Volpone has made of himself. Mosca's case proceeds somewhat differently, for as Volpone appears to degenerate socially, Mosca appears to rise. His proper place in society is that of servant. By his cunning acting he rises to the position of parasite, trusted confidant of a great man and the agent of other great men of the city. Ultimately he occupies Volpone's vacated place and becomes a *magnifico* about to marry into one of the city's great families. But this meteoric rise is all pretense and it finally melts away to the reality of the galley slave, the sentence imposed upon him by the court.

"The way up is the way down," a reverse statement of the religious belief that humility raises a man spiritually, applies to Volpone on the physical and psychic levels as well as the social. His chief disguise throughout the play is that of a sick and dying man, and it requires no particular knowledge of Elizabethan lore or the Great Chain of Being to see that the physical pretense here is the spiritual reality. In his soul Volpone is as sick as he pretends to be in body, and so, ironically, each detail of sickness which Volpone and Mosca work out and act so artfully, instead of

21

covering reality reveals the truth about the man who has sub-
stituted gold for his God and his soul.[9] But over and above this
general irony of disguise built into the play, Volpone is traced
down the scale in considerable detail; and to appreciate this degeneration we must look more closely at the image of man as he
was defined within the Great Chain of Being. The lowest of
human faculties were believed to be those man shares with the
vegetable world: the ability to eat and nourish the body, and to
procreate. Next in order came the faculties shared with the animals, mobility and the five senses. The senses were also ordered
hierarchically, and in general, following Aristotle, sight was considered the highest of the five and touch the lowest. Above the
animal faculties were ranged the rational faculties, which man
shares with the angels, and these were in ascending order: common sense, fancy, memory, and reason. Reason is further
subdivided into the understanding, or wit, and the will. The
understanding permits man to know the good, either inherently
or by acquired knowledge, and the will is the power to choose
the good. The proper way of life for man is, of course, to order
his lower faculties with his higher, and to live, to the degree
possible for so mixed a creature, a life of reason.

In outline the theory is quite simple, and many of us still sub-
scribe to it to some degree, at least sufficiently to understand the
moral judgment of Volpone based on this psychology and ethic.
What Jonson has done in the play, in a general if not a perfectly
systematic manner, is to conduct Volpone, via his disguises,
down this hierarchy of human faculties. His understanding disappears in the opening lines, where he conceives of good as re-
siding in gold, the material world, rather than in the soul and

9. The same technique is used to reveal the lawyer Voltore. In V.12,
where he pretends to be possessed by a devil "in shape of a blue toad with
a bat's wings," the pretense discloses the truth about a lawyer who pleads
so eloquently for falsehood and for gold.

those institutions, religion, and society, which express man's spiritual nature. His will is immediately corrupted, for he chooses gold as his soul and his god with all the fervor of a saint choosing salvation. His higher faculties gone, it is inevitable that he will further degenerate. Common sense disappears at once as he becomes susceptible to the most outrageous flattery and forgets that he is only a mortal man with severe limitations. The remainder of the descent is accomplished by means of the disguise of sickness. Memory soon goes:

> He knows no man,
> No face of friend, nor name of any servant,
> Who 't was that fed him last, or gave him drink;
> Not those he hath begotten, or brought up,
> Can he remember.
>
> (I.5.39–43)

His five senses disappear one by one—and while they may reappear if the situation requires it, the general movement is downward. Sight, the highest of the senses, goes first (I.3.17) and by Act I, Scene 5, he is described as retaining only touch, the lowest of the senses: Mosca advises Corvino to place the pearl he has brought into Volpone's hands because (18–20):

> 'tis only there
> He apprehends, he has his feeling yet.
> See how he grasps it!

In Acts II and III, when Volpone resumes the disguise of sickness, his symptoms reveal even further degeneration. Act I has brought him to the level of the lowest of the animals—the parasite is the usual example given of the animal who has only the sense of touch—but now he falls below the vegetable level as his reproductive and nutritive faculties disappear. Corvino is gulled into believing that there is no danger in lending his beautiful wife to a Volpone so far gone that his sexual powers have disappeared.

"A long forgetfulness hath seized that part," Mosca says, and "nought can warm his blood . . . but a fever" (II.6.64–66). In Act III Corvino assures his wife, Celia, that getting into bed with Volpone involves no danger to her honor because the man is so weak that he can no longer even feed himself:

> An old, decrepit wretch,
> That has no sense, no sinew; takes his meat
> With others' fingers; only knows to gape
> When you do scald his gums; a voice, a shadow . . .
>
> (III.7.42–45)

Below the level of vegetable it would seem impossible for a man to go, but Volpone predicts his own end when he compares himself to a "stone" and to a "dead leaf" (III.7.84–85). By Act IV, when he is brought into the court "as impotent," he has become simply an object to be carried about. The end is inevitable, and Volpone seeks it out with his usual pride in his genius for inventing roles. To instrument a final joke on the fortune hunters he pretends to be dead. His descent from man to mere corrupt matter is hastily completed when Mosca asks what he is to say if anyone should ask what has become of the body:

> *Volpone.* Say it was corrupted.
> *Mosca.* I'll say it stunk, sir; and was fain t' have it
> Coffined up instantly and sent away.
>
> (V.2.77–79)

While Volpone's symptoms are pretenses, they do mirror genuine moral failings. The loss of sight and hearing suggests his moral blindness and deafness. The retention of only the sense of touch is a perfect image of his grossness and materialism: only if you can touch a thing is it real! The failure of reproductive powers reminds us that Volpone has cut himself off from society and from family. His children are those monstrous distortions of nature, the dwarf, the hermaphrodite, the eunuch, and other bastards begotten on "beggars, Gypsies, and Jews, and black-moors when he was drunk" (I.5.44–45). His inability to feed and nourish himself reflects the very real spiritual starvation which he is undergoing, which ends in the death of the soul and the corruption of the body. Greed, lust, selfish individualism, and vulgar materialism are identified with the process of physical decay to mark the "progress" down the ladder of being from man to corruption. And the man chose freely to trace this path, thinking all the while that he was achieving godhead.

The greatness of Jonson's play comes from his ability to bring, by means of irony, two great views of human nature into perfect juxtaposition. On one hand we have a vivid depiction in Volpone and Mosca of an exuberantly sensual delight in the physical world, here symbolized by gold, and a bursting vitality which enables man to believe that by himself he can remake world and man to conform to his own desires—here symbolized by acting. These are views which we take to be characteristic of the Renaissance, and Jonson gives them shape and language which for sheer vitality and evocative power have never been surpassed. The brilliance of phrase and the urgency of rhythms in such speeches as Volpone's praise of his gold and his temptation of Celia guarantee that Jonson himself responded powerfully to this optimism; but he was at the same time the greatest classicist of his age, profoundly committed to the principles of order and tradition in religion, society, and literature. And so he counterweights the joyful worldliness of his characters with a rigid moral system and a vision of reality built up and refined upon by pagan and Christian thinkers over two thousand years. Volpone and the views he represents were, in Jonson's time, only the latest of a long series of challenges to society and established order. They were as contemporary and shining new as a fresh-minted coin, and yet they were as old as Satan himself. And the end was the same in both cases. With the predictable regularity of a machine, each step

part of pervasive spirit of the Renais.

25

upward in defiance of nature becomes a step downward. Mosca perfectly, though unintentionally, describes this specious progress of "your fine elegant rascal," who, he says, "can rise and stoop almost together." And by the end of *Volpone*, despite all attempts to cover truth and all skill at playing, reality asserts itself once more as the impostors' physical shapes are brought into conformity with their true natures. Their own greed unmasks them, and the court locks these Proteans into the shapes they have wrought for themselves: Mosca becomes a perpetual galley slave; Volpone is condemned to prison, where, as a moral incurable, his body will be cramped by irons to fit it to his spiritual diseases; Voltore is exiled from his profession and the state, condemned to wander outside society like the outlaw he truly is; Corbaccio is confined to a monastery and treated as a moral idiot who has forgotten that he has a soul which will be held to account; and Corvino is turned into a civic joke, made to wear a cap with the ears of an ass and sit in the pillory.[10]

10. The subplot has the same kind of conclusion. Sir Politic after pretending to be a clever statesman is forced to confess his pretenses and, driven by his fears, to disguising (revealing) himself as a tortoise.

To the
Most Noble And Most Equal Sisters,
The Two Famous Universities,
For Their
Love and Acceptance Shown to His Poem
In The Presentation;
Ben. Jonson,
The Grateful Acknowledger,
Dedicates Both It And Himself.

There follows an Epistle, if
you dare venture on the length.

Never, most equal Sisters, had any man a wit so presently excellent as that it could raise itself; but there must come both matter,
occasion, commenders, and favorers to it. If this be true, and that
the fortune of all writers doth daily prove it, it behooves the careful to provide well toward these accidents, and, having acquired   5
them, to preserve that part of reputation most tenderly wherein
the benefit of a friend is also defended. Hence is it that I now
render myself grateful and am studious to justify the bounty of
your act, to which, though your mere authority were satisfying,
yet, it being an age wherein poetry and the professors of it hear   10

EQUAL *of equal merit, and in the Latin sense:* aequus, *just.*
TWO FAMOUS UNIVERSITIES *Oxford and Cambridge.*
PRESENTATION N. (*N. refers throughout to corresponding note at end of text.*)
THERE . . . LENGTH *in Quarto only.*

1 WIT *intelligence.* PRESENTLY *immediately.*
2 MATTER *subject matter.*
3 THAT *i.e. "that it be the truth."*
5 TOWARD *for.* ACCIDENTS *chance occurrences, incidental additions to wit rather than innate characteristics.*
7 BENEFIT *kindness, i.e. the "love and acceptance shown to his poem."*
9 MERE *absolute.* SATISFYING *sufficient.*
10 PROFESSORS *practitioners.*

Epistle

so ill on all sides, there will a reason be looked for in the subject.
It is certain, nor can it with any forehead be opposed, that the too
much license of poetasters in this time hath much deformed their
mistress, that, every day, their manifold and manifest ignorance
15 doth stick unnatural reproaches upon her; but for their petulancy
it were an act of the greatest injustice either to let the learned
suffer, or so divine a skill (which indeed should not be attempted
with unclean hands) to fall under the least contempt. For, if men
will impartially, and not asquint, look toward the offices and
20 function of a poet, they will easily conclude to themselves the
impossibility of any man's being the good poet without first
being a good man. He that is said to be able to inform young
men to all good disciplines, inflame grown men to all great
virtues, keep old men in their best and supreme state, or, as
25 they decline to childhood, recover them to their first strength;
that comes forth the interpreter and arbiter of nature, a teacher
of things divine no less than human, a master in manners;
and can alone, or with a few, effect the business of mankind:
this, I take him, is no subject for pride and ignorance to exercise
30 their railing rhetoric upon. But it will here be hastily answered
that the writers of these days are other things: that not only their
manners, but their natures, are inverted, and nothing remaining
with them of the dignity of poet but the abused name, which
every scribe usurps; that now, especially in dramatic, or, as they

10–11 HEAR SO ILL *are spoken of in such an ill manner.*
12 FOREHEAD *assurance, command of countenance.*
13 POETASTERS *petty poets.*
14 MISTRESS *the poetic muse, i.e. poetry.*
15 FOR *because of.* PETULANCY *insolence.*
22 INFORM *form, mold.*
28 EFFECT . . . MANKIND *"perform the proper functions of man."*
29 I TAKE HIM *"as I understand it."*
30 RAILING *abusive.*
34–6 *N.*

28

term it, stage poetry, nothing but ribaldry, profanation, blas- 35
phemy, all license of offense to God and man is practiced. I dare
not deny a great part of this, and am sorry I dare not, because in
some men's abortive features (and would they had never boasted
the light) it is overtrue; but that all are embarked in this bold
adventure for hell is a most uncharitable thought, and, uttered, 40
a more malicious slander. For my particular, I can, and from a
most clear conscience, affirm, that I have ever trembled to think
toward the least profaneness, have loathed the use of such foul
and unwashed bawdry as is now made the food of the scene.
And, howsoever I cannot escape, from some, the imputation of 45
sharpness, but that they will say I have taken a pride, or lust, to
be bitter, and not my youngest infant but hath come into the
world with all his teeth; I would ask of these supercilious politics,
what nation, society, or general order, or state I have provoked?
what public person? whether I have not in all these preserved 50
their dignity, as mine own person, safe? My works are read,
allowed (I speak of those that are entirely mine); look into them.
What broad reproofs have I used? where have I been particular?
where personal? except to a mimic, cheater, bawd, or buffoon,
creatures for their insolencies worthy to be taxed? Yet to which 55
of these so pointingly as he might not either ingenuously

38 ABORTIVE FEATURES *premature and malformed plays—plays are here considered the offspring of the poet.*

44 FOOD *substance.*

46 LUST *liking.*

47 YOUNGEST INFANT *Jonson's recent play,* Sejanus, *which had caused him some difficulty with the authorities.*

48 WITH ALL HIS TEETH *capable of biting, satiric.* N. POLITICS *shrewd persons, with the additional sense of cunning contrivers.*

52 ALLOWED N. THOSE . . . MINE N.

53 BROAD *indecent.*

54 MIMIC *actor or perhaps plagiarist.*

55 TAXED *censured.*

56 POINTINGLY *specifically.*

have confessed or wisely dissembled his disease? But it is not rumour can make men guilty, much less entitle me to other men's crimes. I know that nothing can be so innocently writ or

60 carried, but may be made obnoxious to construction; marry, whilst I bear mine innocence about me, I fear it not. Application is now grown a trade with many, and there are that profess to have a key for the deciphering of everything; but let wise and noble persons take heed how they be too credulous, or give leave

65 to these invading interpreters to be overfamiliar with their fames, who cunningly, and often, utter their own virulent malice under other men's simplest meanings. As for those that will (by faults which charity hath raked up, or common honesty concealed) make themselves a name with the multitude, or (to draw their

70 rude and beastly claps) care not whose living faces they entrench with their petulant styles, may they do it without a rival, for me. I choose rather to lie graved in obscurity than share with them in so preposterous a fame. Nor can I blame the wishes of those severe and wiser patriots, who, providing the hurts these licen-

75 tious spirits may do in a state, desire rather to see fools, and devils, and those antique relics of barbarism retrieved, with all other ridiculous and exploded follies, than behold the wounds of private men, of princes, and nations. For, as Horace makes Trebatius speak, among these,

60 CARRIED *managed*. TO CONSTRUCTION *by interpretation*.
61 APPLICATION *specific identification (of persons and events in plays)*.
62 THERE ARE *there are those*.
66 UTTER *used in the special sense of circulating false money*.
68 RAKED UP *covered over*.
69 MAKE . . . NAME *by insisting that they are caricatured in some play*.
70 CLAPS *applause*. ENTRENCH *mark*.
74 PATRIOTS *those concerned for the nation's welfare*. PROVIDING *foreseeing*.
75 FOOLS, AND DEVILS *N*.
76 ANTIQUE *grotesque*.
77 EXPLODED *literally "to clap and hoot off the stage" OED*.

—Sibi quisque timet, quamquam est intactus, et odit. 80

And men may justly impute such rages, if continued, to the
writer, as his sports. The increase of which lust in liberty, together
with the present trade of the stage, in all their misc'line interludes,
what learned or liberal soul doth not already abhor? where nothing but the filth of the time is uttered, and that with such impro- 85
priety of phrase, such plenty of solecisms, such dearth of sense, so
bold prolepses, so racked metaphors, with brothelry able to vio-
late the ear of a pagan, and blasphemy to turn the blood of a
Christian to water. I cannot but be serious in a cause of this
nature, wherein my fame and the reputations of divers honest 90
and learned are the question; when a name so full of authority,
antiquity, and all great mark, is, through their insolence, become
the lowest scorn of the age; and those men subject to the petulancy of every vernaculous orator that were wont to be the care
of kings and happiest monarchs. This it is that hath not only rapt 95
me to present indignation, but made me studious heretofore, and
by all my actions to stand off from them; which may most appear in this my latest work—which you, most learned Arbitresses,
have seen, judged, and, to my crown, approved—wherein I have
labored, for their instruction and amendment, to reduce not only 100
the ancient forms, but manners of the scene: the easiness, the pro-
priety, the innocence, and last, the doctrine, which is the principal

80 SIBI . . . ODIT *"Although he is uninjured, everyone fears for himself and is
      angry"* (Horace, Sermones 2.1.23).
81-2 THE WRITER N.
82 LUST *pleasure.* LIBERTY *unrestrained freedom.*
83 MISC'LINE *mixed, jumbled.*
91 QUESTION *topic.* A NAME *Horace N.*
92 MARK *note.*
94 VERNACULOUS *ill bred, scurrilous.*
95 RAPT *carried by force.*
100 REDUCE *bring back.*
102 INNOCENCE *harmlessness.*

this version of Sidney's statement — "virtuous action" . . . "teach + delight"

end of poesie, to inform men in the best reason of living. And
though my catastrophe may in the strict rigor of comic law meet
105 with censure, as turning back to my promise; I desire the learned
and charitable critic to have so much faith in me to think it was
done of industry: for with what ease I could have varied it nearer
his scale (but that I fear to boast my own faculty) I could here
insert. But my special aim being to put the snaffle in their mouths
110 that cry out: We never punish vice in our interludes, &c. I took
the more liberty, though not without some lines of example,
drawn even in the ancients themselves, the goings out of whose
comedies are not always joyful, but oft times the bawds, the
servants, the rivals, yea, and the masters are mulcted, and fitly, it
115 being the office of a comic poet to imitate justice, and instruct to
life, as well as purity of language, or stir up gentle affections. To
which I shall take the occasion elsewhere to speak. For the present, most reverenced Sisters, as I have cared to be thankful for
your affections past, and here made the understanding acquainted
120 with some ground of your favors, let me not despair their con-
tinuance, to the maturing of some worthier fruits; wherein, if
my muses be true to me, I shall raise the despised head of poetry
again, and stripping her out of those rotten and base rags wherewith the times have adulterated her form, restore her to her
125 primitive habit, feature, and majesty, and render her worthy to

function of comic poet

his weapon to effort with poetry

104 CATASTROPHE *climax of the play.*
105 AS . . . PROMISE *"because it fails to fulfill my promise (to reduce . . . the ancient forms)"* N.
107 OF INDUSTRY *purposely.*
110 WE . . . INTERLUDES N. INTERLUDES *plays.*
112 GOINGS OUT *conclusions.*
116 AS . . . AFFECTIONS *Jonson's parallelism breaks down in the last two gram-matical elements.* TO *about.*
116–7 TO . . . SPEAK N.
119 THE UNDERSTANDING *the intelligent.*
125 PRIMITIVE *original, first.* HABIT *clothing.*

be embraced and kissed of all the great and master-spirits of our
world. As for the vile and slothful, who never affected an act
worthy of celebration, or are so inward with their own vicious
natures, as they worthily fear her and think it a high point of
policy to keep her in contempt with their declamatory and windy 130
invectives; she shall out of just rage incite her servants (who are
genus irritabile) to spout ink in their faces that shall eat, farther than
their marrow, into their fames, and not Cinnamus the barber
with his art shall be able to take out the brands, but they shall
live, and be read, till the wretches die, as things worst deserving 135
of themselves in chief, and then of all mankind.

From my house in the Blackfriars,
this 11th day of February, 1607

133 CINNAMUS THE BARBER *N.*
134 BRANDS *scars, marks.*
136 IN CHIEF *first of all.*
137–8 FROM . . . 1607 *in quarto only.*
137 BLACKFRIARS *N.*

The Persons of the Play

Volpone, a Magnifico
Mosca, his Parasite
Voltore, an Advocate
Corbaccio, an old Gentleman
Corvino, a Merchant
Avocatori, four Magistrates
Notario, the Register
Nano, a Dwarf
Castrone, an Eunuch
[Sir] Politic Wouldbe, a Knight
Peregrine, a Gent[leman]-traveler
Bonario, a young Gentleman [son of Corbaccio]
Fine Madame Wouldbe, the Knight's wife
Celia, the Merchant's wife
Commendatori, Officers
Mercatori, three Merchants
Androgyno, a Hermaphrodite
Servitore, a servant
Grege
Women

The Scene

Venice

VOLPONE *N.*
MAGNIFICO *rich and distinguished man.*
PARASITE *a flatterer, hanger-on.*
ADVOCATE *lawyer.*
REGISTER *clerk of the court.*
[SIR] POLITIC *"Politic" here has the meaning of crafty and skilled in diplomacy.*
GREGE *crowd.*
VENICE *N.*

34

THE ARGUMENT

V olpone, childless, rich, feigns sick, despairs,
O ffers his state to hopes of several heirs,
L ies languishing; his Parasite receives
P resents of all, assures, deludes; then weaves
O ther cross plots, which ope themselves, are told.   5
N ew tricks for safety are sought; they thrive; when, bold,
E ach tempts th' other again, and all are sold.

2 STATE *property.*
5 OPE *open.* TOLD *exposed.*
7 SOLD *enslaved.*

PROLOGUE

Now, luck yet send us, and a little wit
   Will serve to make our play hit;
According to the palates of the season,
   Here is rhyme not empty of reason.
This we were bid to credit from our poet,
   Whose true scope, if you would know it,
In all his poems still hath been this measure:
   To mix profit with your pleasure;

5 CREDIT *believe, understand.*
6 SCOPE *aim.*
8 TO . . . PLEASURE *the Horatian formula,* utile dulci, *which Jonson refers
   to frequently.*

35

And not as some, whose throats their envy failing,
10   Cry hoarsely, "All he writes is railing,"
And when his plays come forth, think they can flout them,
    With saying, "He was a year about them."
To these there needs no lie but this his creature,
    Which was two months since no feature;
15 And though he dares give them five lives to mend it,
    'Tis known, five weeks fully penned it,
From his own hand, without a coadjutor,
    Novice, journeyman, or tutor.
Yet thus much I can give you as a token
20   Of his play's worth: no eggs are broken,
Nor quaking custards with fierce teeth affrighted,
    Wherewith your rout are so delighted;
Nor hales he in a gull old ends reciting,
    To stop gaps in his loose writing,
25 With such a deal of monstrous and forced action,
    As might make Bedlam a faction;
Nor made he 'his play for jests stol'n from each table,
    But makes jests to fit his fable.

10 RAILING *carping, abusive language.*
12 "HE . . . THEM" N.
13 TO . . . CREATURE *"this play answers the charge."*
14 WAS . . . FEATURE *"was not begun two months ago."*
17–18 COADJUTOR . . . TUTOR N.
21 QUAKING CUSTARDS N.
22 ROUT *mob.*
23 HALES *hauls.* GULL *simple dupe.* OLD ENDS *bits and pieces of poetry—Shake-speare's Pistol is the most remarkable reciter of old ends in Elizabethan drama.*
26 MAKE . . . FACTION *"add a new party to the madhouse"* BEDLAM *St. Mary of Bethlehem, a religious institution which became the London insane asylum.*
27–8 *"He does not construct his plays to accommodate stolen jokes, but makes his own jokes to fit his plays."*
27 STOL'N FROM EACH TABLE N.
28 FABLE *plot.*

And so presents quick comedy refined,
   As best critics have designed;   30
The laws of time, place, persons he observeth,
   From no needful rule he swerveth.
All gall and copperas from his ink he draineth,
   Only a little salt remaineth,
Wherewith he'll rub your cheeks, till red with laughter,   35
   They shall look fresh a week after.

29 QUICK *lively.*
31 LAWS . . . PERSONS *N.*
33 COPPERAS *an acid.*

Act I Scene i

[Volpone's house.]

[Volpone.] Good morning to the day; and next, my gold!
Open the shrine that I may see my saint.

[Mosca opens a curtain disclosing piles of gold.]

Hail the world's soul, and mine! More glad than is
The teeming earth to see the longed-for sun
5   Peep through the horns of the celestial Ram,
Am I, to view thy splendor darkening his;
That lying here, amongst my other hoards,
Show'st like a flame by night, or like the day
Struck out of chaos, when all darkness fled
10 Unto the center. O thou son of Sol,
But brighter than thy father, let me kiss,
With adoration, thee, and every relic
Of sacred treasure in this blessed room.
Well did wise poets by thy glorious name

---

1   *[Volpone]* N.
4   TEEMING *filled with life and ready to bear.*
5   PEEP . . . RAM N.
7   THAT *gold is the understood subject of this clause.*
8–9 DAY . . . CHAOS *the day of creation.*
10 CENTER *center of the earth.* SON OF SOL *in alchemy gold was considered the offspring of the sun.*

38

Title that age which they would have the best,   15
Thou being the best of things, and far transcending
All style of joy in children, parents, friends,
Or any other waking dream on earth.
Thy looks when they to Venus did ascribe,
They should have giv'n her twenty thousand cupids,   20
Such are thy beauties and our loves! Dear saint,
Riches, the dumb god that giv'st all men tongues,
That canst do nought, and yet mak'st men do all things;
The price of souls; even hell, with thee to boot,
Is made worth heaven! Thou art virtue, fame,   25
Honor, and all things else. Who can get thee,
He shall be noble, valiant, honest, wise—
   Mosca. And what he will, sir. Riches are in fortune
A greater good than wisdom is in nature.
   Volpone. True, my belovèd Mosca. Yet, I glory   30
More in the cunning purchase of my wealth
Than in the glad possession, since I gain
No common way: I use no trade, no venture;
I wound no earth with ploughshares; fat no beasts
To feed the shambles; have no mills for iron,   35
Oil, corn, or men, to grind 'em into powder;
I blow no subtle glass; expose no ships

15 THAT AGE *The Age of Gold* N. HAVE *argue to be.*
17 STYLE *form.*
19 THEY . . . ASCRIBE *Venus was frequently styled "golden" (aurea Venus) by
   the Latin poets.*
22 THE DUMB GOD *"silence is golden."*
28 WHAT *whatever.*
31 PURCHASE *getting.*
32 GAIN *make money in.*
33 COMMON *ordinary.* USE *employ.* VENTURE *risky business enterprise.*
35 SHAMBLES *slaughterhouse.*
36 CORN *grain.*
37 SUBTLE *intricately wrought.*

To threat'nings of the furrow-facèd sea;
I turn no monies in the public bank,
40 Nor usure private—
    Mosca.   No, sir, nor devour
Soft prodigals. You shall ha' some will swallow
A melting heir as glibly as your Dutch
Will pills of butter, and ne'er purge for 't;
Tear forth the fathers of poor families
45 Out of their beds, and coffin them, alive,
In some kind, clasping prison, where their bones
May be forthcoming, when the flesh is rotten.
But, your sweet nature doth abhor these courses;
You loathe the widow's or the orphan's tears
50 Should wash your pavements, or their piteous cries
Ring in your roofs, and beat the air for vengeance—
    Volpone. Right, Mosca, I do loathe it.
    Mosca   And, besides, sir,
You are not like the thresher that doth stand
With a huge flail, watching a heap of corn,
55 And, hungry, dares not taste the smallest grain,
But feeds on mallows and such bitter herbs;
Nor like the merchant, who hath filled his vaults
With Romagnìa and rich Candian wines,
Yet drinks the lees of Lombard's vinegar.
60 You will not lie in straw, whilst moths and worms

39 TURN *"to keep passing in a course of exchange or traffic."*
40 USURE N. PRIVATE *privately.*
41 SOFT PRODIGALS *easy spendthrifts.*
42–3 DUTCH . . . BUTTER *The Dutch were famous for their delight in eating butter.*
43 PURGE *take a laxative.*
56 MALLOWS *a variety of coarse, harsh plants.*
58 ROMAGNÌA *wine from Greece (Romanie) often referred to as "Rumney."*
    Note accent on next to last syllable. CANDIAN WINES *from Candy, i.e. Crete.*
59 LOMBARD'S VINEGAR *cheap, acid wine from Lombardy.*

Feed on your sumptuous hangings and soft beds.
You know the use of riches, and dare give, now,
From that bright heap, to me, your poor observer,
Or to your dwarf, or your hermaphrodite,
Your eunuch, or what other household trifle
Your pleasure allows maintenance—   65

    Volpone.   Hold thee, Mosca,   [*Gives*
Take, of my hand; thou strik'st on truth in all,   *him money.*]
And they are envious term thee parasite.
Call forth my dwarf, my eunuch, and my fool,
And let 'em make me sport. What should I do   [*Exit Mosca.*] 70
But cocker up my genius and live free
To all delights my fortune calls me to?
I have no wife, no parent, child, ally,
To give my substance to; but whom I make
Must be my heir, and this makes men observe me.   75
This draws new clients, daily, to my house,
Women and men of every sex and age,
That bring me presents, send me plate, coin, jewels,
With hope that when I die (which they expect
Each greedy minute) it shall then return   80
Tenfold upon them; whilst some, covetous
Above the rest, seek to engross me, whole,
And counterwork the one unto the other,
Contend in gifts, as they would seem in love.

68 TERM *that term.*
71 COCKER UP *encourage.* GENIUS *innate talents.*
74 WHOM I MAKE *whomever I designate.*
75 OBSERVE *be obsequious to.*
76 CLIENTS *followers N.*
78 PLATE *dishes and utensils made of silver or gold.*
82 ENGROSS *to absorb entirely.*
83 UNTO *against.*
84 AS . . . LOVE *"in order to try to show that they love me."*

85 All which I suffer, playing with their hopes,
   And am content to coin 'em into profit,
   And look upon their kindness, and take more,
   And look on that; still bearing them in hand,
   Letting the cherry knock against their lips,
90 And draw it by their mouths, and back again,
   How now!

85 SUFFER *allow*.
88 BEARING . . . HAND *leading them on*.

Act I Scene ii

[*Mosca enters with Nano, Androgyno, and Castrone prepared to put on an entertainment.*]

Nano. Now, room for fresh gamesters, who do will you to
    know,
They do bring you neither play nor university show;
And therefore do entreat you that whatsoever they rehearse,
May not fare a whit the worse, for the false pace of the verse.
5 If you wonder at this, you will wonder more ere we pass,
For know, here is enclosed the soul of Pythagoras, [*Pointing
That juggler divine, as hereafter shall follow;   to Androgyno.*]
Which soul, fast and loose, sir, came first from Apollo,
And was breathed into Aethalides, Mercurius his son,

1 N.
2 PLAY . . . SHOW N.
4 FALSE PACE *referring to the doggerel rhythms and forced rhymes of this speech.*
6 PYTHAGORAS *Greek philosopher of 6th century* B.C., *and founder of a school which had for one of its tenets a belief in transmigration, the passage of the soul from one body to another after death.*
8 FAST AND LOOSE N.
9 AETHALIDES *herald for Jason's Argonauts.* MERCURIUS HIS *a common Elizabethan form of third person singular possessive.*

42

Where it had the gift to remember all that ever was done.   10
From thence it fled forth, and made quick transmigration
To goldy-locked Euphorbus, who was killed in good fashion,
At the siege of old Troy, by the cuckold of Sparta.
Hermotimus was next (I find it in my charta)
To whom it did pass, where no sooner it was missing,   15
But with one Pyrrhus of Delos it learned to go afishing;
And thence did it enter the sophist of Greece.
From Pythagore, she went into a beautiful piece,
Hight Aspasia, the meretrix; and the next toss of her
Was again of a whore, she became a philosopher,   20
Crates the Cynic, as itself doth relate it.
Since, kings, knights, and beggars, knaves, lords, and fools gat it,
Besides ox and ass, camel, mule, goat, and brock,
In all which it hath spoke, as in the Cobbler's cock.
But I come not here to discourse of that matter,   25
Or his one, two, or three, or his great oath, "By Quater!"
His musics, his trigon, his golden thigh,

12 EUPHORBUS *the Trojan who first wounded Patroclus,* Iliad *17.*
13 CUCKOLD OF SPARTA *Menelaus, whose wife, Helen, was stolen by Paris.*
14 HERMOTIMUS *a Greek philosopher of Claizomene who lived about 500 B.C.*
   CHARTA *paper; either the part he is reading or the source of this information,*
   Lucian's "Dialogue of the Cobbler and the Cock."
16 PYRRHUS OF DELOS. *This could be one of several classical philosophers.*
17 SOPHIST *philosopher—Pythagoras is meant.*
19 ASPASIA *the mistress of Pericles, leader of Athens in the 5th century.* MERETRIX
   courtesan.
21 CRATES *Crates of Thebes, a pupil of the Cynic philosopher Diogenes.* ITSELF
   the neuter pronoun suggests that Nano may here point to Androgyno who is
   playing the part of the soul.
23 BROCK *badger.*
24 COBBLER'S COCK *the cock who speaks in Lucian's dialogue. See note to line 1.*
26 "BY QUATER" N.
27 TRIGON *triangle.* GOLDEN THIGH *Pythagoras was believed by his followers to*
   have had a golden thigh.

A = 20rl

Act I Scene ii

Or his telling how elements shift; but I
Would ask, how of late thou hast suffered translation,
30 And shifted thy coat in these days of reformation?
    Androgyno. Like one of the reformèd, a fool, as you see,
Counting all old doctrine heresy.
    Nano. But not on thine own forbid meats hast thou ventured?
    Androgyno. On fish, when first a Carthusian I entered.
35   *Nano.* Why, then thy dogmatical silence hath left thee?
    Androgyno. Of that an obstreperous lawyer bereft me.
    Nano. O wonderful change! When Sir Lawyer forsook thee,
For Pythagore's sake, what body then took thee?
    Androgyno. A good, dull moyle. *(mule)*
    Nano.   And how! by that means
40 Thou wert brought to allow of the eating of beans?
    Androgyno. Yes.
    Nano.   But from the moyle into whom didst thou
    pass?
    Androgyno. Into a very strange beast, by some writers called an
    ass;
By others, a precise, pure, illuminate brother,
Of those devour flesh, and sometimes one another,
45 And will drop you forth a libel, or a sanctified lie,
Betwixt every spoonful of a nativity pie.

29 TRANSLATION *change, transmigration.*
30 REFORMATION *i.e. The Protestant Reformation.*
31 REFORMÈD *Puritans.*
33 FORBID MEATS *forbidden foods—the Pythagoreans did not eat fish.*
34 CARTHUSIAN *a religious order famed for the severity of its diet.*
35 SILENCE *the Pythagoreans were bound to a five-year silence.*
36 OBSTREPEROUS *in the Latin sense, "to make a noise."*
39 MOYLE *mule.*
43 PRECISE *Puritanical.* ILLUMINATE *illuminated, i.e. one who has had a vision of religious truth.*
46 NATIVITY PIE *Christmas pie.*

44

Nano. Now quit thee, for heaven, of that profane nation,
And gently report thy next transmigration.
   Androgyno. To the same that I am.
   Nano.   A creature of delight,
And what is more than a fool, an hermaphrodite?   50
Now, 'pray thee, sweet soul, in all thy variation,
Which body wouldst thou choose to take up thy station?
   Androgyno. Troth, this I am in, even here would I tarry.
   Nano. 'Cause here the delight of each sex thou canst vary?
   Androgyno. Alas, those pleasures be stale and forsaken;   55
No, 'tis your fool wherewith I am so taken,
The only one creature that I can call blessèd,
For all other forms I have proved most distressèd.
   Nano. Spoke true, as thou wert in Pythagoras still.
This learned opinion we celebrate will,   60
Fellow eunuch, as behooves us, with all our wit and art,
To dignify that whereof ourselves are so great and special a part.
   Volpone. Now, very, very pretty! Mosca, this
Was thy invention?
   Mosca.   If it please my patron,
Not else.
   Volpone. It doth, good Mosca.
   Mosca.   Then it was, sir.   65

Song

Fools, they are the only nation
Worth men's envy or admiration;
Free from care or sorrow-taking,

47 QUIT THEE *get out.*
52 TO . . . STATION *to stay in.*
53 TROTH *in truth.*
62 THAT *i.e. folly.*
65 SONG *Volpone and Mosca may join the three grotesques in this song, or the
latter may sing it alone as a conclusion to their entertainment.*

45

Selves and others merry making,
70   All they speak or do is sterling.
Your fool, he is your great man's dearling,
And your ladies' sport and pleasure;
Tongue and bable are his treasure.
E'en his face begetteth laughter,
75   And he speaks truth free from slaughter.
He's the grace of every feast,
And, sometimes, the chiefest guest:
Hath his trencher and his stool,
When wit waits upon the fool.
80   O, who would not be
            Hee, hee, hee?

One knocks without.

Volpone. Who's that? Away! Look, Mosca.
Mosca.   Fool, begone!

[*Exeunt Nano, Castrone, Androgyno.*]
'Tis Signior Voltore, the advocate;
I know him by his knock.
      Volpone.   Fetch me my gown,
85 My furs, and night-caps; say my couch is changing,
And let him entertain himself awhile
Without i' th' gallery. [*Exit Mosca.*] Now, now, my clients
Begin their visitation! Vulture, kite,
Raven, and gorcrow, all my birds of prey,

70 STERLING *excellent.*
71 DEARLING *darling.*
73 BABLE *bauble, the mock scepter carried by a jester or professional fool—also slang for the male organ. The word also suggests "babble."*
75 FREE FROM SLAUGHTER *without fear of consequences. For rhyming of "laughter" and "slaughter" see N.*
85 FURS *warm robes worn by the sick man.* MY COUCH IS CHANGING *my bed is being changed.*
89 GORCROW *carrion crow.*

That think me turning carcass, now they come.   90
I am not for 'em yet. [*Enter Mosca.*]
                   How now? the news?
  Mosca. A piece of plate, sir.
  Volpone.   Of what bigness?
  Mosca.   Huge,
Massy, and antique, with your name inscribed,
And arms engraven.
  Volpone.   Good! and not a fox
Stretched on the earth, with fine delusive sleights   95
Mocking a gaping crow? ha, Mosca!
  Mosca.   Sharp, sir.
  Volpone. Give me my furs. Why dost thou laugh so, man?
  Mosca. I cannot choose, sir, when I apprehend
What thoughts he has, without, now, as he walks:
That this might be the last gift he should give;   100
That this would fetch you; if you died today,
And gave him all, what he should be tomorrow;
What large return would come of all his ventures;
How he should worshipped be, and reverenced;
Ride with his furs, and foot-cloths; waited on   105
By herds of fools and clients; have clear way
Made for his moyle, as lettered as himself;
Be called the great and learnèd advocate:
And then concludes, there's nought impossible.
  Volpone. Yes, to be learnèd, Mosca.
  Mosca.   O, no; rich   110
Implies it. Hood an ass with reverend purple,

91 FOR 'EM *ready for them, i.e. not yet "made up" as a dying man.*

103 VENTURES *business enterprises; specifically here, the gifts he has given Volpone.*

107 LETTERED *learned.*

111 HOOD . . . PURPLE *the purple hood worn on the academic gown by Doctors of Philosophy.*

So you can hide his two ambitious ears,
And he shall pass for a cathedral doctor.
   Volpone. My caps, my caps, good Mosca. Fetch him in.
   Mosca. Stay, sir; your ointment for your eyes.
115 *Volpone.*   That's true;
Dispatch, dispatch. I long to have possession
Of my new present.
   Mosca.   That, and thousands more,
I hope to see you lord of.
   Volpone.   Thanks, kind Mosca.
   Mosca. And that, when I am lost in blended dust,
120 And hundreds such as I am, in succession—
   Volpone. Nay, that were too much, Mosca.
   Mosca.   You shall live
Still to delude these harpies.
   Volpone.   Loving Mosca!
                      [*Looking into a mirror.*]
'Tis well. My pillow now, and let him enter.   [*Exit Mosca.*]
Now, my feigned cough, my phthisic, and my gout,
125 My apoplexy, palsy, and catarrhs,
Help, with your forcèd functions, this my posture,
Wherein, this three year, I have milked their hopes.
He comes, I hear him—uh! uh! uh! uh! O—

115 OINTMENT . . . EYES *to make them look rheumy.*
116 DISPATCH *hurry.*
120 IN SUCCESSION *following me, i.e. other servants to Volpone.*
122 STILL *always.*
123 'TIS . . . NOW *Volpone is satisfied with the make-up and costume he has,
like an actor, been donning. He now settles into his sick bed.* N.
124–7 NOW . . . HOPES *N.*
124 PHTHISIC *consumption.*
126 POSTURE *imposture.*
127 THIS THREE YEAR *for three years.*

Act I Scene iii

[*Enter Mosca with Voltore. Volpone in bed.*]
    Mosca. You still are what you were, sir. Only you,
Of all the rest, are he commands his love,
And you do wisely to preserve it thus,
With early visitation, and kind notes
Of your good meaning to him, which, I know,   5
Cannot but come most grateful. Patron, sir.
Here's Signior Voltore is come—
    Volpone. [*faintly.*]   What say you?
    Mosca. Sir, Signior Voltore is come this morning
To visit you.
    Volpone.   I thank him.
    Mosca.   And hath brought
A piece of antique plate, bought of St. Mark,   10
With which he here presents you.
    Volpone.   He is welcome.
Pray him to come more often.
    Mosca.   Yes.
    Voltore.   What says he?
    Mosca. He thanks you and desires you see him often.
    Volpone. Mosca.
    Mosca.   My patron?
    Volpone.   Bring him near, where is he?
I long to feel his hand.

  2 ARE HE *are that man.*
  5 GOOD MEANING *well wishing.*
10 OF ST. MARK *at a goldsmith's shop in the Square of St. Mark.*
12 WHAT SAYS HE *throughout this scene Volpone speaks in a very low voice, and
pretends that he can neither see nor hear very well.*

15   *Mosca.* [*directing Volpone's groping hands.*] The plate is here, sir.

     Voltore. How fare you, sir?

     Volpone.   I thank you, Signior Voltore. Where is the plate? mine eyes are bad.

     Voltore. [*putting it into his hands.*]   I'm sorry To see you still thus weak.

     Mosca.   [*Aside.*] That he is not weaker.

     Volpone. You are too munificent.

     Voltore.   No, sir; would to heaven
20 I could as well give health to you as that plate!

     Volpone. You give, sir, what you can. I thank you. Your love Hath taste in this, and shall not be unanswered. I pray you see me often.

     Voltore.   Yes, I shall, sir.

     Volpone. Be not far from me.

     Mosca. [*to Voltore.*]   Do you observe that, sir?
25 *Volpone.* Hearken unto me still; it will concern you.

     Mosca. You are a happy man, sir; know your good.

     Volpone. I cannot now last long—

     Mosca.   You are his heir, sir.

     Voltore. Am I?

     Volpone.   I feel me going, uh! uh! uh! uh! I am sailing to my port, uh! uh! uh! uh!
30 And I am glad I am so near my haven.

     Mosca. Alas, kind gentleman. Well, we must all go—

     Voltore. But, Mosca—

     Mosca.   Age will conquer.

     Voltore.   Pray thee, hear me. Am I inscribed his heir for certain?

21–2 YOUR . . . THIS "*this (the plate) gives an idea of how much you love me.*"
22 UNANSWERED *unrewarded.*

Mosca.   Are you?
I do beseech you, sir, you will vouchsafe
To write me i' your family. All my hopes   35
Depend upon your worship. I am lost
Except the rising sun do shine on me.
    Voltore. It shall both shine and warm thee, Mosca.
    Mosca.   Sir,
I am a man that have not done your love
All the worst offices. Here I wear your keys,   40
See all your coffers and your caskets locked,
Keep the poor inventory of your jewels,
Your plate, and monies; am your steward, sir,
Husband your goods here.
    Voltore.   But am I sole heir?
    Mosca. Without a partner, sir, confirmed this morning;   45
The wax is warm yet, and the ink scarce dry
Upon the parchment.
    Voltore.   Happy, happy me!
By what good chance, sweet Mosca?
    Mosca.   Your desert, sir;
I know no second cause.
    Voltore.   Thy modesty
Is loth to know it; well, we shall requite it.   50
    Mosca. He ever liked your course, sir; that first took him.
I oft have heard him say how he admired
Men of your large profession, that could speak
To every cause, and things mere contraries,
Till they were hoarse again, yet all be law;   55

35 TO . . . FAMILY *"make me a member of your household."*
51 COURSE *manner of acting.* TOOK HIM *took his fancy.*
53 LARGE *liberal.*
53–4 SPEAK . . . CONTRARIES *defend any case and argue for exactly opposite causes.*
54 MERE *absolute.*

51

seems to praise him
but comments
are satire

That, with most quick agility, could turn,
And re-turn; make knots, and undo them;
Give forkèd counsel; take provoking gold
On either hand, and put it up. These men,
60 He knew, would thrive with their humility.
And, for his part, he thought he should be bless'd
To have his heir of such a suffering spirit,
So wise, so grave, of so perplexed a tongue,
And loud withal, that would not wag, nor scarce
65 Lie still, without a fee; when every word
Your worship but lets fall, is a chequin! *Another knocks.*
Who's that? One knocks. I would not have you seen, sir.
And yet—pretend you came and went in haste;
I'll fashion an excuse. And, gentle sir,
70 When you do come to swim in golden lard,
Up to the arms in honey, that your chin
Is borne up stiff with fatness of the flood,
Think on your vassal; but remember me:
I ha' not been your worst of clients.
     Voltore.   Mosca—
75 *Mosca.* When will you have your inventory brought, sir?
Or see a copy of the will? [*Calling out to the one knocking.*] Anon.
I'll bring 'em to you, sir. Away, be gone,
Put business i' your face.   [*Exit Voltore.*]
     Volpone.   Excellent, Mosca!
Come hither, let me kiss thee.

58 FORKÈD *fork-tongued.* PROVOKING *"provoke . . . To call to a judge or court to take up one's cause"* (OED).
59 PUT IT UP *pocket it.*
63 PERPLEXED *intricate (in the sense of being double, speaking on either side).*
66 CHEQUIN *a gold coin.*
73 BUT *simply.*
78 PUT . . . FACE *"look as if you were here on a matter of business."*

[Handwritten at top: Vltare = vulture; Corbaccio = raven]

Mosca.   Keep you still, sir.
Here is Corbaccio.
    Volpone.   Set the plate away.   80
The vulture's gone, and the old raven's come.

Act I Scene iv

    Mosca. Betake you to your silence, and your sleep.
[*Sets the plate aside.*] Stand there and multiply. Now shall we see
A wretch who is indeed more impotent
Than this can feign to be, yet hopes to hop
Over his grave. [*Enter Corbaccio.*] Signior Corbaccio!   5
You're very welcome, sir.
    Corbaccio.   How does your patron?
    Mosca. Troth, as he did, sir; no amends.
    Corbaccio. [*cupping his ear.*]   What? mends he?
    Mosca. [*shouting.*] No, sir. He is rather worse.
    Corbaccio.   That's well. Where is he?

[Handwritten margin note: deafness as anger device]

    Mosca. Upon his couch, sir, newly fall'n asleep.
    Corbaccio. Does he sleep well?
    Mosca.   No wink, sir, all this night,   10
Nor yesterday, but slumbers.
    Corbaccio.   Good! he should take
Some counsel of physicians. I have brought him
An opiate here, from mine own doctor—
    Mosca. He will not hear of drugs.
    Corbaccio.   Why? I myself
Stood by while 't was made, saw all th' ingredients,   15

4 THIS *Volpone.*
11 BUT SLUMBERS *only dozes.*

And know it cannot but most gently work.
My life for his, 'tis but to make him sleep.
    Volpone. [*Aside.*] Ay, his last sleep, if he would take it.
    Mosca.   Sir,
He has no faith in physic.
    Corbaccio.   Say you, say you?
20   *Mosca.* He has no faith in physic: he does think
Most of your doctors are the greater danger,
And worse disease t' escape. I often have
Heard him protest that your physician
Should never be his heir.
    Corbaccio.   Not I his heir?
25   *Mosca.* Not your physician, sir.
    Corbaccio.   O, no, no, no,
I do not mean it.
    Mosca.   No, sir, nor their fees
He cannot brook; he says they flay a man
Before they kill him.
    Corbaccio.   Right, I do conceive you.
    Mosca. And then, they do it by experiment,
30 For which the law not only doth absolve 'em,
But gives them great reward; and he is loth
To hire his death so.
    Corbaccio.   It is true, they kill
With as much license as a judge.
    Mosca.   Nay, more;
For he but kills, sir, where the law condemns,

19 PHYSIC *medicine.*
21 YOUR *used not to refer to Corbaccio's doctor, but in vague and contemptuous reference to doctors in general.*
26 MEAN *intend.*
27 FLAY *skin alive.*
28 CONCEIVE *understand.*
29 BY EXPERIMENT *by trying out various remedies on the patient.*

And these can kill him too.
    Corbaccio.   Ay, or me,   35
Or any man. How does his apoplex?
Is that strong on him still?
    Mosca.   Most violent.
His speech is broken, and his eyes are set,
His face drawn longer than 't was wont—
    Corbaccio.   How! how!
Stronger than he was wont?
    Mosca.   No, sir; his face
Drawn longer than 't was wont.
    Corbaccio.   O, good.
    Mosca.   His mouth
Is ever gaping, and his eyelids hang.
    Corbaccio.   Good.
    Mosca. A freezing numbness stiffens all his joints,
And makes the color of his flesh like lead.
    Corbaccio.   'Tis good.
    Mosca. His pulse beats slow and dull.
    Corbaccio.   Good symptoms still.   45
    Mosca. And from his brain—
    Corbaccio.   Ha! How? not from his brain?
    Mosca. Yes, sir, and from his brain—
    Corbaccio.   I conceive you; good.
    Mosca. Flows a cold sweat, with a continual rheum,
Forth the resolvèd corners of his eyes.
    Corbaccio. Is't possible? Yet I am better, ha!   50
How does he with the swimming of his head?
    Mosca. O, sir, 'tis past the scotomy; he now
Hath lost his feeling, and hath left to snort;

46 FROM HIS BRAIN *N.*
49 RESOLVÈD *relaxed.*
52 SCOTOMY *dimness of sight accompanied by dizziness.*
53 LEFT *ceased.*

You hardly can perceive him that he breathes.

55   *Corbaccio.* Excellent, excellent; sure I shall outlast him!
This makes me young again, a score of years.
    Mosca. I was a-coming for you, sir.
    Corbaccio.   Has he made his will?
What has he given me?
    Mosca.   No, sir.
    Corbaccio.   Nothing? ha!
    Mosca. He has not made his will, sir.
    Corbaccio.   Oh, oh, oh.

60 What then did Voltore, the lawyer, here?
    Mosca. He smelled a carcass, sir, when he but heard
My master was about his testament;
As I did urge him to it for your good—
    Corbaccio. He came unto him, did he? I thought so.

65   *Mosca.* Yes, and presented him this piece of plate.
    Corbaccio. To be his heir?
    Mosca.   I do not know, sir.
    Corbaccio.   True,
I know it too.
    Mosca. [*Aside*] By your own scale, sir.
    Corbaccio.   Well,
I shall prevent him yet. See, Mosca, look,
Here I have brought a bag of bright chequins,
70 Will quite weigh down his plate.

54 PERCEIVE HIM THAT *perceive that.*
56 THIS . . . YEARS "*This news makes me feel twenty years younger.*"
66–7 TRUE . . . TOO *Corbaccio pays no attention to what Mosca says, or does
not hear him, and assumes that he has agreed that Voltore came to be made
heir.*
67 BY . . . SCALE "*measuring by your own standard.*"
68 PREVENT *get ahead of—literally* "*come before.*"
70 WEIGH DOWN *outweigh in scales.* MARRY *indeed.*

Mosca. [taking the bag]   Yea, marry, sir.   70
This is true physic, this your sacred medicine;
No talk of opiates to this great elixir.
     Corbaccio. 'Tis aurum palpabile, if not potabile.
     Mosca. It shall be ministered to him, in his bowl?
     Corbaccio. Ay, do, do, do.
     Mosca.   Most blessed cordial!   75
This will recover him.
     Corbaccio.   Yes, do, do, do.
     Mosca. I think it were not best, sir.
     Corbaccio.   What?
     Mosca.   To recover him.
     Corbaccio. O, no, no, no; by no means.
     Mosca.   Why, sir, this
Will work some strange effect if he but feel it.
     Corbaccio. 'Tis true, therefore forbear; I'll take my venture;   80
Give me 't again.
     Mosca.   At no hand. Pardon me.
You shall not do yourself that wrong, sir. I
Will so advise you, you shall have it all.
     Corbaccio. How?
     Mosca.   All, sir; 'tis your right, your own; no man
Can claim a part; 'tis yours without a rival,   85
Decreed by destiny.
     Corbaccio.   How, how, good Mosca?
     Mosca. I'll tell you, sir. This fit he shall recover—
     Corbaccio. I do conceive you.

---

72 NO . . . TO "*There is no comparing other medicines to . . .*" ELIXIR *a drug*
     supposed to be capable of prolonging life indefinitely.
73 AURUM PALPABILE *gold which can be felt.* POTABILE *drinkable N.*
75 CORDIAL *a medicine which stimulates the heart.*
80 VENTURE *i.e. the bag of gold.*
87 RECOVER *recover from.*

    Mosca.   And on first advantage
Of his gained sense, will I re-importune him
90 Unto the making of his testament,
And show him this. [*Points to the bag of gold.*]
    Corbaccio.   Good, good.
    Mosca.   'Tis better yet,
If you will hear, sir.
    Corbaccio.   Yes, with all my heart.
    Mosca. Now would I counsel you, make home with speed;
There, frame a will whereto you shall inscribe
95 My master your sole heir.
    Corbaccio.   And disinherit
My son?
    Mosca. O, sir, the better; for that color
Shall make it much more taking.
    Corbaccio.   O, but color?
    Mosca. This will, sir, you shall send it unto me.
Now, when I come to enforce, as I will do,
100 Your cares, your watchings, and your many prayers,
Your more than many gifts, your this day's present,
And, last, produce your will; where, without thought
Or least regard unto your proper issue,
A son so brave and highly meriting,
105 The stream of your diverted love hath thrown you
Upon my master, and made him your heir:
He cannot be so stupid, or stone dead,
But out of conscience and mere gratitude—

88 FIRST ADVANTAGE *first opportunity.*
89 GAINED *regained.*
94 FRAME *devise, write.* WHERETO *wherein.*
96 COLOR *pretense, outward appearance concealing truth.*
97 TAKING *attractive.* O, BUT COLOR? "*O, is it only pretense?*"
99 ENFORCE *urge.*
103 PROPER ISSUE *true child.*
108 MERE *complete.*

Corbaccio. He must pronounce me his?

Mosca.   'Tis true.

Corbaccio.   This plot
Did I think on before.

Mosca.   I do believe it.   110

Corbaccio. Do you not believe it?

Mosca.   Yes, sir.

Corbaccio.   Mine own project.

Mosca. Which, when he hath done, sir—

Corbaccio.   Published me his heir?

Mosca. And you so certain to survive him—

Corbaccio   Ay.

Mosca. Being so lusty a man—

Corbaccio.   'Tis true.

Mosca.   Yes, sir—

Corbaccio. I thought on that too. See, how he should be   115
The very organ to express my thoughts!

Mosca. You have not only done yourself a good—

Corbaccio. But multiplied it on my son?

Mosca.   'Tis right, sir.

Corbaccio. Still my invention.

Mosca.   'Las, sir, heaven knows
It hath been all my study, all my care,   120
(I e'en grow grey withal) how to work things—

Corbaccio. I do conceive, sweet Mosca.

Mosca.   You are he
For whom I labor here.

Corbaccio.   Ay, do, do, do.

110 THINK ON BEFORE *think of earlier.*
115 SEE . . . BE *"Look, and if he isn't . . ."*
116 VERY ORGAN *exact instrument.*
119 STILL MY INVENTION! *"Again my idea!"* (?) 'LAS *Alas*
120 STUDY *concern.*

Act I Scene iv

I'll straight about it. [*Going.*]

[*Mosca now begins to bow and smile while speaking too softly for Corbaccio to hear.*]

Mosca.   Rook go with you, raven!

125 Corbaccio. I know thee honest.

Mosca.   You do lie, sir.

Corbaccio.   And—

Mosca. Your knowledge is no better than your ears, sir.

Corbaccio. I do not doubt to be a father to thee.

Mosca. Nor I to gull my brother of his blessing.

Corbaccio. I may ha' my youth restored to me, why not?

130 Mosca. Your worship is a precious ass—

Corbaccio.   What sayst thou?

Mosca. I do desire your worship to make haste, sir.

Corbaccio. 'Tis done, 'tis done, I go.   [*Exit.*]

Volpone. [*Leaping up.*]   O, I shall burst!

Let out my sides, let out my sides.

Mosca.   Contain

Your flux of laughter, sir. You know this hope

135 Is such a bait it covers any hook.

Volpone. O, but thy working, and thy placing it!

I cannot hold; good rascal, let me kiss thee.

I never knew thee in so rare a humor.

Mosca. Alas, sir, I but do as I am taught;

140 Follow your grave instructions; give 'em words;

---

124 STRAIGHT *at once*. ROOK GO WITH YOU "*May you be cheated (rooked).*"

126 YOUR . . . EARS "*Your understanding is no better than your hearing*"—*referring to Corbaccio's deafness and perhaps suggesting that being an ass, he has the ears of that animal.*

128 GULL *cheat*. MY BROTHER *Corbaccio's son. N.*

134 FLUX *flood—the word also means "dysentery."* THIS HOPE *i.e. to inherit Volpone's wealth.*

138 RARE *excellent*. HUMOR *fanciful mood.*

140 GRAVE *wise.*

60

Pour oil into their ears, and send them hence.

    Volpone. 'Tis true, 'tis true. What a rare punishment   ⟨*ironic for him to say*⟩
Is avarice to itself!

    Mosca.   Ay, with our help, sir.

    Volpone. So many cares, so many maladies,
So many fears attending on old age.   145
Yea, death so often called on as no wish
Can be more frequent with 'em. Their limbs faint,
Their senses dull, their seeing, hearing, going,
All dead before them; yea, their very teeth,
Their instruments of eating, failing them.   150
Yet this is reckoned life! Nay, here was one,
Is now gone home, that wishes to live longer!
Feels not his gout, nor palsy; feigns himself
Younger by scores of years, flatters his age
With confident belying it; hopes he may   155
With charms, like Aeson have his youth restored;
And with these thoughts so battens, as if fate
Would be as easily cheated on as he,   *Another knocks.*
And all turns air! Who's that, there, now? a third?

    Mosca. Close to your couch again; I hear his voice.   160
It is Corvino, our spruce merchant.

    Volpone. [*Lies down.*]   Dead.

    Mosca. Another bout, sir, with your eyes. Who's there?

141 POUR . . . EARS *flatter them with soft, easy words.*
148 GOING *ability to walk.*
149 BEFORE THEM *before they are.*
152 IS (*who*) *is.*
156 AESON *N.*
157 BATTENS *grows fat.*
159 ALL TURNS AIR *everything becomes nothing.*
162 BOUT *turn––Mosca again puts ointment in Volpone's eyes.*

Act I Scene v

[*Enter Corvino.*]

Mosca. Signior Corvino! come most wished for! O,
How happy were you, if you knew it, now!

Corvino. Why? what? wherein?

Mosca.   The tardy hour is come, sir.

Corvino. He is not dead?

Mosca.   Not dead, sir, but as good;
5 He knows no man.

Corvino.   How shall I do then?

Mosca.   Why, sir?

Corvino. I have brought him here a pearl.

Mosca.   Perhaps he has
So much remembrance left as to know you, sir.
He still calls on you, nothing but your name
Is in his mouth. Is your pearl orient, sir?

10 *Corvino.* Venice was never owner of the like.

Volpone. [*Faintly.*] Signior Corvino.

Mosca.   Hark.

Volpone.   Signior Corvino.

Mosca. He calls you; step and give it him. He is here, sir.
And he has brought you a rich pearl.

Corvino.   How do you, sir?
Tell him it doubles the twelfth caract.

Mosca.   Sir,
15 He cannot understand, his hearing's gone,
And yet it comforts him to see you—

  1 COME MOST "*arrived, just when you are most . . .*"
  9 ORIENT *precious and lustrous.*
  14 CARACT *carat.*

62

Corvino.   Say
I have a diamond for him, too.
    Mosca.   Best show 't, sir,
Put it into his hand; 'tis only there
He apprehends, he has his feeling yet. [*Volpone seizes the pearl.*]
See how he grasps it!
    Corvino.   'Las, good gentleman.   20
How pitiful the sight is!
    Mosca.   Tut, forget, sir.
The weeping of an heir should still be laughter
Under a visor.
    Corvino.   Why, am I his heir?
    Mosca. Sir, I am sworn, I may not show the will
Till he be dead. But here has been Corbaccio,   25
Here has been Voltore, here were others too,
I cannot number 'em, they were so many;
All gaping here for legacies; but I,
Taking the vantage of his naming you,
"*Signior Corvino, Signior Corvino,*" took   30
Paper, and pen, and ink, and there I asked him
Whom he would have his heir? "*Corvino.*" Who
Should be executor? "*Corvino.*" And
To any question he was silent to,
I still interpreted the nods he made,   35
Through weakness, for consent; and sent home th' others,
Nothing bequeathed them but to cry and curse. *They embrace.*
    Corvino. O, my dear Mosca. Does he not perceive us?
    Mosca. No more than a blind harper. He knows no man,

17 DIAMOND *trisyllabic: di-a-mond.*
23 VISOR *mask.*
30 SIGNIOR CORVINO *Mosca imitates Volpone's feeble voice.*
35 STILL *continually.*
39 BLIND HARPER *proverbial term for member of a crowd.*

40 No face of friend, nor name of any servant,
Who 't was that fed him last, or gave him drink;
Not those he hath begotten, or brought up,
Can he remember.
    Corvino.   Has he children?
    Mosca.   Bastards,
Some dozen, or more, that he begot on beggars,
45 Gypsies, and Jews, and black-moors when he was drunk.
Knew you not that, sir? 'Tis the common fable,
The dwarf, the fool, the eunuch are all his;
He's the true father of his family,
In all save me, but he has given 'em nothing.
50   *Corvino.* That's well, that's well. Art sure he does not hear us?
    Mosca. Sure, sir? why, look you, credit your own sense.
                             [*Shouts in Volpone's ear.*]
The pox approach and add to your diseases,
If it would send you hence the sooner, sir,
For, your incontinence, it hath deserved it
55 Throughly and throughly, and the plague to boot.
You may come near, sir—Would you would once close
Those filthy eyes of yours that flow with slime
Like two frog-pits, and those same hanging cheeks,
Covered with hide instead of skin—Nay, help, sir—
60 That look like frozen dish-clouts set on end.
    Corvino. Or, like an old smoked wall, on which the rain
Ran down in streaks.

46 FABLE *story—not used here in the modern sense of* "*something invented or made up.*"
52 POX *the great pox, i.e. syphilis.*
54 IT . . . IT *incontinence . . . the pox.*
55 THROUGHLY . . . THROUGHLY *through and through.*
56 YOU . . . SIR *Mosca speaks here to Corvino.*
58 FROG-PITS *stagnant puddles in which frogs live.*
60 CLOUTS *rags.*

Mosca.   Excellent, sir, speak out.
You may be louder yet; a culverin
Dischargèd in his ear would hardly bore it.
     Corvino. His nose is like a common sewer, still running.   65
     Mosca. 'Tis good! And what his mouth?
     Corvino.   A very draught.
     Mosca. O, stop it up— [*Starting to smother him.*]
     Corvino.   By no means.
     Mosca.   Pray you, let me.
Faith I could stifle him rarely with a pillow,
As well as any woman that should keep him.
     Corvino. Do as you will, but I'll be gone.
     Mosca.   Be so.   70
It is your presence makes him last so long.
     Corvino. I pray you, use no violence.
     Mosca.   No, sir? why?
Why should you be thus scrupulous, pray you, sir?
     Corvino. Nay, at your discretion.
     Mosca.   Well, good sir, be gone.
     Corvino. I will not trouble him now to take my pearl?   75
     Mosca. Puh! nor your diamond. What a needless care
                           [*Taking the jewels.*]
Is this afflicts you! Is not all here yours?
Am not I here, whom you have made? Your creature?
That owe my being to you?
     Corvino.   Grateful Mosca!
Thou art my friend, my fellow, my companion,
My partner, and shalt share in all my fortunes.   80
     Mosca. Excepting one.

63 CULVERIN *musket or a cannon.*
68 RARELY *excellently.*
73 SCRUPULOUS *overly nice.*
75 PEARL *Volpone has the pearl and diamond clutched in his hand.*

Act I Scene v

    Corvino.   What's that?
    Mosca.   Your gallant wife, sir.
                             [*Exit Corvino hurriedly.*]

Now is he gone; we had no other means
To shoot him hence but this.
    Volpone.   My divine Mosca!
85 Thou hast today outgone thyself. *Another knocks.*
                            Who's there?
I will be troubled with no more. Prepare
Me music, dances, banquets, all delights;
The Turk is not more sensual in his pleasures
Than will Volpone. [*Exit Mosca.*]
                     Let me see: a pearl!
90 A diamond! plate! chequins! good morning's purchase.
Why, this is better than rob churches, yet,
Or fat, by eating once a month a man. [*Enter Mosca.*]
Who is 't?
    Mosca.   The beauteous Lady Wouldbe, sir,
Wife to the English knight, Sir Politic Wouldbe—
95 This is the style, sir, is directed me—
Hath sent to know how you have slept tonight,
And if you would be visited?
    Volpone.   Not now.
Some three hours hence.—
    Mosca.   I told the squire so much.
    Volpone. When I am high with mirth and wine, then, then.
100 'Fore heaven, I wonder at the desperate valor

88 TURK *the Turks were noted for their extreme sensuality as well as their
    cruelty.*
90 PURCHASE *catch.*
92 FAT *grow fat.*
95 STYLE *manner of speaking.* IS DIRECTED ME *"that I am ordered to use."*
100–3 *N.*

Of the bold English, that they dare let loose
Their wives to all encounters!
   Mosca.   Sir, this knight
Had not his name for nothing; he is *politic*,
And knows, howe'er his wife affect strange airs,
She hath not yet the face to be dishonest.   105
But had she Signior Corvino's wife's face—
   Volpone. Has she so rare a face?
   Mosca.   O, sir, the wonder,
The blazing star of Italy, a wench
O' the first year! a beauty ripe as harvest!
Whose skin is whiter than a swan, all over!   110
Than silver, snow, or lilies! a soft lip,
Would tempt you to eternity of kissing!
And flesh that melteth in the touch to blood!
Bright as your gold! and lovely as your gold!
   Volpone. Why had not I known this before?
   Mosca.   Alas, sir,   115
Myself but yesterday discovered it.
   Volpone. How might I see her?
   Mosca.   O, not possible;
She's kept as warily as is your gold,
Never does come abroad, never takes air
But at a window. All her looks are sweet   120
As the first grapes or cherries, and are watched
As near as they are.
   Volpone.   I must see her—
   Mosca.   Sir,
There is a guard, of ten spies thick, upon her;

105 DISHONEST *unchaste.*
109 O' THE FIRST YEAR *of the finest order.*
113 TO BLOOD *to blushes.*
119 ABROAD *out of the house.*
122 NEAR *closely.*

67

Act I Scene v

All his whole household; each of which is set
125 Upon his fellow, and have all their charge,
When he goes out, when he comes in, examined.
    Volpone. I will go see her, though but at her window.
    Mosca. In some disguise then.
    Volpone.   That is true. I must
Maintain mine own shape still the same: we'll think.
                    [Exeunt.]

124–5 SET UPON *set to watch.*
125 CHARGE *responsibility.*
126 HE *Corvino N.*
129 MAINTAIN . . . SHAPE *N.*

Act II Scene i

[*The Public Square, before Corvino's House.*]
[*Enter Politic Wouldbe, Peregrine.*]

Sir Politic. Sir, to a wise man, all the world's his soil.
It is not Italy, nor France, nor Europe,
That must bound me, if my fates call me forth.
Yet, I protest, it is no salt desire
Of seeing countries, shifting a religion,   5
Nor any disaffection to the state
Where I was bred, and unto which I owe
My dearest plots, hath brought me out; much less
That idle, antique, stale, grey-headed project
Of knowing men's minds, and manners, with Ulysses;   10
But a peculiar humor of my wife's,
Laid for this height of Venice, to observe,
To quote, to learn the language, and so forth.

1 SOIL *country.*

4 SALT *keen.*

6 DISAFFECTION TO *dissatisfaction with.*

8 PLOTS *schemes, projects.*

10 ULYSSES *N.*

11 HUMOR *passion.*

12 LAID . . . HEIGHT *aimed for the latitude. Sir Politic uses an elaborate manner of speech, and avoids the plain word whenever he can.*

13 QUOTE *note down (the peculiarities of the country).*

I hope you travel, sir, with license?

    Peregrine.   Yes.

15   *Sir Politic.* I dare the safelier converse. How long, sir,

Since you left England?

    Peregrine.   Seven weeks.

    Sir Politic.   So lately!

You ha' not been with my lord ambassador?

    Peregrine. Not yet, sir.

    Sir Politic.   'Pray you, what news, sir, vents our

    climate?

I heard, last night, a most strange thing reported

20 By some of my lord's followers, and I long

To hear how 'twill be seconded.

    Peregrine.   What was't, sir?

    Sir Politic. Marry, sir, of a raven, that should build

In a ship royal of the King's.

    Peregrine.   [*Aside.*] —This fellow,

Does he gull me, trow? or is gulled?—Your name, sir?

25 *Sir Politic.* My name is Politic Wouldbe.

    Peregrine.   [*Aside.*] —O, that speaks him—

A knight, sir?

    Sir Politic. A poor knight, sir.

    Peregrine.   Your lady

Lies here, in Venice, for intelligence

---

14 LICENSE *passport.*

17 MY LORD AMBASSADOR N.

18 VENTS OUR CLIMATE *comes from our country. Another of Sir Pol's circum-*
locutions.

21 SECONDED *confirmed.*

22 RAVEN *bird of ill omen.* SHOULD *used here to mark reported speech.*

24 GULL *fool.* TROW *a mild expletive.*

25 SPEAKS *defines.*

27 LIES *stays.* INTELLIGENCE *knowledge.*

Of tires, and fashions, and behavior
Among the courtesans? The fine Lady Wouldbe?
   Sir Politic. Yes, sir, the spider and the bee ofttimes   30
Suck from one flower.
   Peregrine.   Good Sir Politic!
I cry you mercy; I have heard much of you.
'Tis true, sir, of your raven.
   Sir Politic.   On your knowledge?
   Peregrine. Yes, and your lion's whelping in the Tower. {was a real lion in the tower}
   Sir Politic. Another whelp!
   Peregrine.   Another, sir.
   Sir Politic.   Now heaven!   35
What prodigies be these? The fires at Berwick!
And the new star! These things concurring, strange!
And full of omen! Saw you those meteors?
   Peregrine. I did, sir.
   Sir Politic.   Fearful! Pray you, sir, confirm me,
Were there three porpoises seen above the bridge,   40
As they give out?
   Peregrine.   Six, and a sturgeon, sir.
   Sir Politic. I am astonished!
   Peregrine.   Nay, sir, be not so;
I'll tell you a greater prodigy than these—

28 TIRES *attires, clothes.*
29 COURTESANS *fashionable prostitutes. Venice was famous for its courtesans.*
32 CRY YOU MERCY *"ask your pardon" (for not recognizing you).*
33 YOUR *used indeterminately, or to mean roughly, "that you know of."*
34 LION'S . . . TOWER N.
36 PRODIGIES *strange omens.*
36–7 FIRES . . . STAR N.
37 CONCURRING *coinciding.*
38 METEORS N.
40 THE BRIDGE *London Bridge.*
41 GIVE OUT *report.*

71

Sir Politic. What should these things portend?

Peregrine.   The very day
45 (Let me be sure) that I put forth from London,
There was a whale discovered in the river,
As high as Woolwich, that had waited there,
Few know how many months, for the subversion
Of the Stode fleet.

Sir Politic.   Is't possible? Believe it,
50 'Twas either sent from Spain, or the Archduke's!
Spinola's whale, upon my life, my credit!
Will they not leave these projects? Worthy sir,
Some other news.

Peregrine.   Faith, Stone the fool is dead,
And they do lack a tavern fool extremely.
55 *Sir Politic.* Is Mas' Stone dead?

Peregrine.   He's dead, sir; why, I hope
You thought him not immortal? [*Aside.*] —O, this knight,
Were he well known, would be a precious thing
To fit our English stage. He that should write
But such a fellow, should be thought to feign
60 Extremely, if not maliciously.—

Sir Politic.   Stone dead!

Peregrine. Dead. Lord, how deeply, sir, you apprehend it!
He was no kinsman to you?

Sir Politic.   That I know of.

---

46 WHALE N.
49 STODE *city at the mouth of the Elbe.*
50 ARCHDUKE *ruler of the Spanish Netherlands.*
51 SPINOLA N.
53 STONE N.
55 MAS' *master.*
61 APPREHEND *both "feel" and "understand."*
62 THAT *not that.*

Well, that same fellow was an unknown fool.
    Peregrine. And yet you know him, it seems?
    Sir Politic.   I did so. Sir,
I knew him one of the most dangerous heads   65
Living within the state, and so I held him.
    Peregrine. Indeed, sir?
    Sir Politic.   While he lived, in action.
He has received weekly intelligence,
Upon my knowledge, out of the Low Countries,
For all parts of the world, in cabbages;   70
And those dispensed, again, t' ambassadors,
In oranges, musk-melons, apricots,
Lemons, pome-citrons, and suchlike; sometimes
In Colchester oysters, and your Selsey cockles.
    *Peregrine.*You make me wonder.
    Sir Politic.   Sir, upon my knowledge.   75
Nay, I have observed him at your public ordinary
Take his advertisement from a traveler,
A concealed statesman, in a trencher of meat;
And, instantly, before the meal was done,
Convey an answer in a toothpick.
    Peregrine.   Strange!   80
How could this be, sir?
    Sir Politic.   Why, the meat was cut

---

63 UNKNOWN *misinterpreted.*
65 DANGEROUS HEADS *subversive persons.*
67 ACTION *doing—i.e. he was an active spy, not merely passively unfriendly to the state.*
73 POME-CITRONS *lemon-like fruit.*
76 ORDINARY *tavern.*
77 ADVERTISEMENT *information.*
78 CONCEALED STATESMAN *disguised agent.* TRENCHER *platter.*
80 TOOTHPICK *N.*

Act II Scene i

So like his chàracter, and so laid as he
Must easily read the cipher.

    Peregrine.   I have heard
He could not read, sir.

    Sir Politic.   So 'twas given out,
85 In policy, by those that did employ him;
But he could read, and had your languages,
And to 't, as sound a noddle—

    Peregrine.   I have heard, sir,
That your baboons were spies, and that they were
A kind of subtle nation near to China.

    90 *Sir Politic.* Ay, ay, your Mamuluchi. Faith, they had
Their hand in a French plot, or two; but they
Were so extremely given to women as
They made discovery of all; yet I
Had my advices here, on Wednesday last,
95 From one of their own coat, they were returned,
Made their relations, as the fashion is,
And now stand fair for fresh employment.

    Peregrine.   [*Aside.*] —'Heart!
This Sir Pol will be ignorant of nothing—
It seems, sir, you know all.

82 CHARACTER *handwriting, code—accented on second syllable, cha-ràc-ter.*
85 POLICY *craft.*
86 HAD . . . LANGUAGES *was a skilled linguist.*
87 TO 'T *in addition.* NODDLE *head, intelligence.*
89 SUBTLE *cunning and devious.*
90 MAMULUCHI *N.*
92 GIVEN TO *fond of.*
93 DISCOVERY *disclosure.*
94 ADVICES *dispatches.*
95 COAT *party, faction.*
96 RELATIONS *reports.*
97 STAND FAIR *are ready.* 'HEART *God's Heart; curses were frequently formed in this manner, e.g. 'swounds, God's wounds.*

    Sir Politic.   Not all, sir. But
I have some general notions; I do love   100
To note and to observe: though I live out,
Free from the active torrent, yet I'd mark
The currents and the passages of things
For mine own private use; and know the ebbs
And flows of state.
    Peregrine.   Believe it, sir, I hold   105
Myself in no small tie unto my fortunes
For casting me thus luckily upon you,
Whose knowledge, if your bounty equal it,
May do me great assistance in instruction
For my behavior, and my bearing, which   110
Is yet so rude and raw.
    Sir Politic.   Why? came you forth
Empty of rules for travel?
    Peregrine.   Faith, I had
Some common ones, from out that vulgar grammar,
Which he that cried Italian to me, taught me.
    Sir Politic. Why, this it is that spoils all our brave bloods,   115
Trusting our hopeful gentry unto pedants,
Fellows of outside, and mere bark. You seem
To be a gentleman, of ingenuous race—

101–2 THOUGH . . . TORRENT *"though I am not actively engaged in political affairs."*
106 IN . . . TIE *much obliged.*
108 IF . . . IT *"if you are as generous as you are wise."*
113 VULGAR GRAMMAR *ordinary grammar book.*
114 CRIED *pronounced, i.e. taught.*
115 BRAVE BLOODS *gallants, well-born young men.*
117 OUTSIDE . . . BARK *mere show and pretense—"bark" seems also to be a poor pun going back to "cried."*
118 INGENUOUS RACE *noble lineage.*

I not profess it, but my fate hath been
120 To be where I have been consulted with
In this high kind, touching some great men's sons,
Persons of blood and honor—
    Peregrine.   Who be these, sir?

119 I . . . IT "*It* [*the education of high-born young men*] *is not my profession.*"
121 HIGH KIND *important matter.* TOUCHING *bearing on.*
122 BLOOD *nobility.*

Act II Scene ii

[*Enter Mosca and Nano, disguised as Mountebank's attendants, with materials to erect a scaffold stage. A crowd follows them.*]
    Mosca. Under that window, there 't must be. The same.
    Sir Politic. Fellows to mount a bank! Did your instructor
In the dear tongues, never discourse to you
Of the Italian mountebanks?
    Peregrine.   Yes, sir.
    Sir Politic.   Why,
5 Here shall you see one.
    Peregrine.   They are quacksalvers,
Fellows that live by venting oils and drugs.
    Sir Politic. Was that the character he gave you of them?
    Peregrine. As I remember.
    Sir Politic.   Pity his ignorance.
They are the only knowing men of Europe!
10 Great general scholars, excellent physicians,

SD *N.*
2 BANK *N.*
3 DEAR *esteemed.*
6 VENTING *vending.*

76

Most admired statesmen, professed favorites
And cabinet counselors to the greatest princes!
The only languaged men of all the world!
  Peregrine. And I have heard they are most lewd impostors,
Made all of terms and shreds; no less beliers   15
Of great men's favors than their own vile medicines;
Which they will utter upon monstrous oaths,
Selling that drug for twopence, ere they part,
Which they have valued at twelve crowns before.
  Sir Politic. Sir, calumnies are answered best with silence. 20
Yourself shall judge. Who is it mounts, my friends?
  Mosca. Scoto of Mantua, sir.
  Sir Politic.   Is't he? Nay, then
I'll proudly promise, sir, you shall behold
Another man than has been phantasied to you.
I wonder, yet, that he should mount his bank
Here, in this nook, that has been wont t'appear   25
In face of the Piazza! Here he comes
        [*Enter Volpone, disguised as a Mountebank.*]
  Volpone. [*to Nano.*] Mount, zany.
  Grege.   Follow, follow, follow, fol-
    low, follow.
        [*Volpone mounts the stage.*]

12 CABINET COUNSELORS *close advisers.*
14 LEWD *ignorant.*
15 TERMS *technical expressions.* SHREDS *bits and pieces of language such as pro-*
    verbs, quotations from the classics.
15–16 BELIERS . . . FAVORS *men who lie about the esteem in which they are held*
    by the great.
17 UTTER *sell.*
22 SCOTO OF MANTUA *N.*
24 PHANTASIED *fancied, presented to the imagination.*
27 IN FACE OF *in the front, or main, part.*
28 ZANY *clown—see note to line 52 below.*

77

Act II Scene ii

Sir Politic. See how the people follow him! He's a man
30 May write ten thousand crowns in bank here. Note,
Mark but his gesture. I do use to observe
The state he keeps in getting up!
Peregrine.   'Tis worth it, sir.
Volpone. Most noble gentlemen, and my worthy patrons, it
may seem strange that I, your Scoto Mantuano, who was
35   ever wont to fix my bank in face of the public Piazza, near
the shelter of the Portico to the Procuratia, should now, after
eight months' absence from this illustrious city of
Venice, humbly retire myself into an obscure nook of the
Piazza.
Sir Politic. Did not I now object the same?
Peregrine.   Peace, sir.
40 *Volpone.* Let me tell you: I am not, as your Lombard proverb
saith, cold on my feet, or content to part with my commodities at a cheaper rate than I accustomed. Look not for
it. Nor that the calumnious reports of that impudent detrac-
tor, and shame to our profession, Allessandro Buttone I
45   mean, who gave out, in public, I was condemned *a sforzato*
to the galleys, for poisoning the Cardinal Bembo's—cook,
hath at all attached, much less dejected me. No, no, worthy
gentlemen; to tell you true, I cannot endure to see the rabble

32 STATE *formality of bearing.*
36 PROCURATIA *residence, along the north side of the Piazza del San Marco, for
the Procurators, important civic officials.* N.
39 OBJECT *bring before the eyes, visualize—another of Sir Pol's extravagant
words.*
41 COLD ON MY FEET *Aver freddo a 'piedi, "to have cold at the feet," be
forced to sell cheap.*
44 BUTTONE *a rival mountebank.*
45 SFORZATO *galley slave.*
46 BEMBO'S—*the dash suggests that Volpone is about to say "mistress."* N.
47 ATTACHED *caused me to be arrested (?).*

78

of these ground *ciarlitani* that spread their cloaks on the pavement as if they meant to do feats of activity, and then come 50 in lamely with their moldy tales out of Boccaccio, like stale Tabarin, the fabulist: some of them discoursing their travels, and of their tedious captivity in the Turk's galleys, when, indeed, were the truth known, they were the Christian's galleys, where very temperately they eat bread, and drunk 55 water, as a wholesome penance enjoined them by their confessors, for base pilferies.

Sir Politic. Note but his bearing and contempt of these.

Volpone. These turdy-facy-nasty-paty-lousy-fartical rogues, with one poor groatsworth of unprepared antimony, finely 60 wrapped up in several *scartoccios*, are able, very well, to kill their twenty a week, and play; yet these meager, starved spirits, who have half stopped the organs of their minds with earthy oppilations, want not their favorers among your shriveled salad-eating artisans, who are overjoyed that they 65 may have their half-pe'rth of physic; though it purge 'em into another world, 't makes no matter.

49 GROUND CIARLITANI *literally "ground charlatans," i.e. the poorer quacks who performed on the pavement rather than on a platform.*

50 FEATS OF ACTIVITY *tumbling.*

51–52 BOCCACCIO . . . FABULIST *N.*

52 TABARIN *a famous zany in an Italian traveling company of comedians—the name means "short cloak."* DISCOURSING *talking of.*

55 EAT *ate.*

56 ENJOINED THEM *prescribed for them.*

60 UNPREPARED *not made fit for human use.*

61 SEVERAL *separate.* SCARTOCCIOS *papers—used to contain medicines, but may here refer also to plays. See N. to line 36.*

63–4 STOPPED . . . OPPILATIONS *"have become so concerned with gross, mundane activities that their minds have ceased to work."* OPPILATIONS *obstructions.*

65 SALAD *probably has meaning here of "raw, unprepared vegetables."* ARTISANS *workers.*

66 HALF-PE'RTH *half-pennyworth.* PHYSIC *medicine.*

Sir Politic. Excellent! ha' you heard better language, sir?

Volpone. Well, let 'em go. And, gentlemen, honorable gentle-
70   men, know that for this time our bank, being thus removed
from the clamors of the *canaglia*, shall be the scene of pleasure
and delight; for I have nothing to sell, little or nothing to sell.

Sir Politic. I told you, sir, his end.

Peregrine. You did so, sir.

75 *Volpone.* I protest, I and my six servants are not able to make
of this precious liquor so fast as it is fetched away from my
lodging by gentlemen of your city, strangers of the Terra
Firma, worshipful merchants, ay, and senators too, who,
ever since my arrival, have detained me to their uses by their
80   splendidous liberalities. And worthily. For what avails your
rich man to have his magazines stuft with *moscadelli*, or of the
purest grape, when his physicians prescribe him, on pain of
death, to drink nothing but water cocted with aniseeds?
O health! health! the blessing of the rich! the riches of the
85   poor! who can buy thee at too dear a rate, since there is no
enjoying this world without thee? Be not then so sparing of
your purses, honorable gentlemen, as to abridge the natural
course of life—

Peregrine. You see his end?

Sir Politic.   Ay, is't not good?

90 *Volpone.* For, when a humid flux, or catarrh, by the mutability
of air falls from your head into an arm or shoulder, or any
other part, take you a ducat, or your chequin of gold, and

71 CANAGLIA canaille, *rabble.*
77–8 TERRA FIRMA *Venetian possessions on the mainland.*
80 WORTHILY *properly.*
81 MAGAZINES *storehouses.* MOSCADELLI *muscatel wines.*
83 COCTED *boiled.*
89 END *goal.*
90 FLUX *catarrh, discharge,* N.

apply to the place affected: see, what good effect it can work. No, no, 'tis this blessed *unguento*, this rare extraction, that hath only power to disperse all malignant humors that pro-   95 ceed either of hot, cold, moist, or windy causes—

Peregrine. I would he had put in dry too.

Sir Politic.   'Pray you, observe.

Volpone. To fortify the most indigest and crude stomach, ay, were it of one that through extreme weakness vomited blood, applying only a warm napkin to the place, after the   100 unction and fricace; for the vertigine in the head, putting but a drop into your nostrils, likewise behind the ears; a most sovereign and approved remedy: the *mal caduco*, cramps, convulsions, paralyses, epilepsies, *tremor cordia*, retired nerves, ill vapours of the spleen, stoppings of the liver, the stone, the   105 strangury, *hernia ventosa*, *iliaca passio*; stops a *dysenteria* im- mediately; easeth the torsion of the small guts; and cures *melancholia hypocondriaca*, being taken and applied according to my printed receipt. (*Pointing to his bill and his glass.*) For, this is the physician, this the medicine; this counsels, this   110 cures; this gives the direction, this works the effect; and, in sum, both together may be termed an abstract of the theoric and practic in the Aesculapian art. 'Twill cost you eight

94 UNGUENTO *salve.*

95 HUMORS *see N. to line 90.*

98 CRUDE *sour.*

101 FRICACE *massage.* VERTIGINE *dizziness. Volpone is now simply reeling off medical jargon in the manner of a pitchman. For glosses on the unfamiliar diseases listed here see N.*

109 RECEIPT *recipe.*

SD BILL *prescription.* GLASS *bottle containing medicine.*

110 THIS . . . THIS *he points first to the bill and then to the glass.*

112 ABSTRACT *compendium.*

THEORIC *theory.*

113 PRACTIC *practice.*

AESCULAPIAN ART *medicine. Aesculapius was the Roman god of medicine.*

115   crowns. And, Zan Fritada, pray thee sing a verse, extempore, in honor of it.

Sir Politic. How do you like him, sir?

Peregrine.   Most strangely, I!

Sir Politic. Is not his language rare?

Peregrine.   But alchemy

I never heard the like, or Broughton's books.

Song .

    Had old Hippocrates or Galen,

120   That to their books put med'cines all in,

    But known this secret, they had never,

    Of which they will be guilty ever,

    Been murderers of so much paper,

    Or wasted many a hurtless taper.

125   No Indian drug had e'er been famèd,

    Tobacco, sassafras not namèd;

    Ne yet of guacum one small stick, sir,

    Nor Raymond Lully's great elixir.

    Ne had been known the Danish Gonswart,

130   Or Paracelsus, with his long sword.

114 ZAN FRITADA *a famous Italian comedian. The order is probably addressed to Nano, who is playing zany to Volpone's mountebank.*

117 BUT *except for.*

118 BROUGHTON'S BOOKS N.

119 HIPPOCRATES OR GALEN *two famous Greek physicians.*

124 HURTLESS *harmless.*

126 TOBACCO, SASSAFRAS *both used as medicines.*

127 NE *nor.* GUACUM *drug extracted from resin of guacium tree.*

128 RAYMOND LULLY *renowned medieval alchemist supposed to have discovered the elixir.*

    ELIXIR *a drug believed by alchemists to be capable of prolonging life and health indefinitely.*

129 GONSWART N.

130 PARACELSUS . . . LONG SWORD N.

Peregrine. All this, yet, will not do; eight crowns is high.

Volpone. No more. Gentlemen, if I had but time to discourse
to you the miraculous effects of this my oil, surnamed *Oglio
del Scoto*, with the countless catalogue of those I have cured
of th'aforesaid, and many more diseases; the patents and 135
privileges of all the princes and commonwealths of Christen-
dom; or but the depositions of those that appeared on my
part, before the signiory of the *Sanita* and most learned college of physicians; where I was authorized, upon notice
taken of the admirable virtues of my medicaments, and 140
mine own excellency in matter of rare and unknown secrets,
not only to disperse them publicly in this famous city, but in
all the territories that happily joy under the government of
the most pious and magnificent states of Italy. But may some
other gallant fellow say, "O, there be divers that make 145
profession to have as good and as experimented receipts as
yours." Indeed, very many have assayed, like apes, in imitation of that, which is really and essentially in me, to make
of this oil; bestowed great cost in furnaces, stills, alembics,
continual fires, and preparation of the ingredients (as indeed 150
there goes to it six hundred several simples, besides some
quantity of human fat, for the conglutination, which we buy
of the anatomists), but, when these practitioners come to
the last decoction, blow, blow, puff, puff, and all flies in

133-4 OGLIO DEL SCOTO *"Dr. Scoto's Oil."*
135 PATENTS *official certificates conferring certain rights.*
136 PRIVILEGE *special ordinance giving honors to an individual.*
138 SIGNIORY . . . SANITA *Venetian board for granting medical licenses.*
145 DIVERS *many.*
146 EXPERIMENTED *tested.*
149 FURNACES, STILLS, ALEMBICS *pieces of alchemical equipment.*
151 SEVERAL SIMPLES *separate herbs.*
154 DECOCTION *boiling to extract the essences.*
BLOW . . . PUFF *Volpone is imitating the alchemist blowing on his fire to get
it to the proper heat.*

155   fumo. Ha, ha, ha! Poor wretches! I rather pity their folly
and indiscretion than their loss of time and money; for those
may be recovered by industry; but to be a fool born is a disease incurable. For myself, I always from my youth have
endeavoured to get the rarest secrets, and book them, either
160   in exchange or for money; I spared nor cost nor labor where
anything was worthy to be learned. And gentlemen, honorable gentlemen, I will undertake, by virtue of chemical art,
out of the honorable hat that covers your head to extract the
four elements, that is to say, the fire, air, water, and earth,
165   and return you your felt without burn or stain. For, whilst
others have been at the balloo, I have been at my book, and
am now past the craggy paths of study, and come to the
flowery plains of honor and reputation.

Sir Politic. I do assure you, sir, that is his aim.

170   Volpone. But to our price—

Peregrine.   And that withal, Sir Pol.

Volpone. You all know, honorable gentlemen, I never valued
this *ampulla*, or vial, at less than eight crowns, but for this
time I am content to be deprived of it for six; six crowns is
the price, and less in courtesy I know you cannot offer me;
175   take it or leave it, howsoever, both it and I am at your

155 FUMO *smoke.*
158 FROM *since.*
159 BOOK *note.*
160 IN EXCHANGE *by trading (secret for secret).*
     NOR . . . NOR *neither . . . nor.*
162 CHEMICAL *alchemical.*
164 FOUR ELEMENTS *see N. to line 90 above.*
166 BALLOO *a Venetian game in which a large ball was tossed high in
the air.*
     AT MY BOOK *in careful study.*
170 WITHAL *as well.*
172 AMPULLA *container.*

service. I ask you not as the value of the thing, for then I
should demand of you a thousand crowns; so the Cardinals
Montalto, Farnese, the great Duke of Tuscany, my gossip,
with divers other princes have given me; but I despise
money. Only to show my affection to you, honorable 180
gentlemen, and your illustrious state here, I have neglected
the messages of these princes, mine own offices, framed my
journey hither, only to present you with the fruits of my
travels. [*To Nano and Mosca.*] Tune your voices once more
to the touch of your instruments, and give the honorable 185
assembly some delightful recreation.

 Peregrine. What monstrous and most painful circumstance
Is here, to get some three or four gazets!
Some threepence i' th' whole, for that 'twill come to.

Song

  You that would last long, list to my song,   190
  Make no more coil, but buy of this oil.
  Would you be ever fair? and young?
  Stout of teeth? and strong of tongue?
  Tart of palate? quick of ear?
  Sharp of sight? of nostril clear?   195
  Moist of hand? and light of foot?
  Or I will come nearer to't,

176 AS THE VALUE *as (the oil) is valued; what it is worth.*
178 GOSSIP *godfather.*
182 OFFICES *duties.*
 FRAMED *directed.*
187 PAINFUL CIRCUMSTANCE *careful arrangement of details, i.e. setting the
 scene in preparation for the sale.*
188 GAZETS *Venetian coin worth a penny.*
189 I' TH' WHOLE *altogether.*
191 COIL *row, fuss.*
194 TART *keen*
197 COME NEARER TO'T *"get down to what is most important."*

Would you live free from all diseases?
Do the act your mistress pleases,
200   Yet fright all aches from your bones?
Here's a med'cine for the nones.

Volpone. Well, I am in a humor, at this time, to make a present
of the small quantity my coffer contains to the rich, in courtesy, and to the poor, for God's sake. Wherefore, now mark:
205   I asked you six crowns, and six crowns at other times you
have paid me; you shall not give me six crowns, nor five,
nor four, nor three, nor two, nor one; nor half a ducat; no,
nor a *moccenigo*. Six-pence it will cost you, or six hundred
pound—expect no lower price, for by the banner of my
210   front, I will not bate a bagatine; that I will have, only,
a pledge of your loves, to carry something from amongst
you to show I am not contemned by you. Therefore, now,
toss your handkerchiefs, cheerfully, cheerfully; and be advertised that the first heroic spirit that deigns to grace me
215   with a handkerchief, I will give it a little remembrance of
something beside, shall please it better than if I had presented it with a double pistolet.

Peregrine. Will you be that heroic spark, Sir Pol?

200 ACHES *disyllabic, "aitches."*
201 NONES *nonce, occasion.*
202 HUMOR *mood.*
208 MOCCENIGO *small coin.*
209–10 BANNER . . . FRONT *the mountebank's banner displayed before his
stand which lists diseases and cures.*
210 BATE *abate, subtract.*
     ONLY *alone.*
212 CONTEMNED *despised.*
213–14 BE ADVERTISED *understand.*
215 IT *him.*
217 DOUBLE PISTOLET *valuable Spanish gold coin.*
218 SPARK *man of fashion.*

Celia at the window throws down her handkerchief ⌐

O see! the window has prevented you.

    Volpone. Lady, I kiss your bounty, and for this timely grace 220
you have done your poor Scoto of Mantua, I will return
you, over and above my oil, a secret of that high and inestim-
able nature shall make you forever enamored on that minute
wherein your eye first descended on so mean, yet not altogether to be despised, an object. Here is a poulder concealed 225
in this paper of which, if I should speak to the worth, nine
thousand volumes were but as one page, that page as a line,
that line as a word: so short is this pilgrimage of man, which
some call life, to the expressing of it. Would I reflect on the
price? Why, the whole world were but as an empire, that 230
empire as a province, that province as a bank, that bank as
a private purse to the purchase of it. I will, only, tell you:
it is the poulder that made Venus a goddess (given her by
Apollo), that kept her perpetually young, cleared her
wrinkles, firmed her gums, filled her skin, colored her hair. 235
From her derived to Helen, and at the sack of Troy unfor-
tunately lost; till now, in this our age, it was as happily
recovered by a studious antiquary out of some ruins of Asia,
who sent a moiety of it to the court of France (but much
sophisticated), wherewith the ladies there now color their 240

hair. The rest, at this present, remains with me; extracted to a quintessence, so that wherever it but touches in youth it perpetually preserves, in age restores the complexion; seats your teeth, did they dance like virginal jacks, firm as a wall; makes them white as ivory, that were black as—

245

241-2 EXTRACTED . . . QUINTESSENCE "*refined to its pure essence.*"
244 VIRGINAL JACKS N.

Act II Scene iii

[*Enter Corvino*]

Corvino. [*Shouting up to Celia.*]
Spite o' the devil, and my shame! [*To Volpone.*] Come down here;
Come down! No house but mine to make your
scene?   He beats
Signior Flaminio, will you down, sir? down?   away the
What, is my wife your Franciscina, sir?   mountebank, &c.
5 No windows on the whole Piazza, here,
To make your properties, but mine? but mine?
Heart! ere tomorrow I shall be new christened,
And called the Pantolone di Besogniosi
About the town.   [*Exit.*]
     Peregrine.   What should this mean, Sir Pol?
10   Sir Politic. Some trick of state, believe it. I will home.
     Peregrine. It may be some design on you.

1 SPITE . . . DEVIL "*manifestation of the devil's hatred of man,*" i.e. *woman.*
2 SCENE N.
3-8 FLAMINIO . . . FRANCISCINA . . . PANTALONE N.
6 PROPERTIES *stage properties, set.*
10 HOME *go home.*
11 DESIGN *plot.*

Sir Politic. I know not.
I'll stand upon my guard.
    Peregrine. It is your best, sir.
    Sir Politic. This three weeks all my advices, all my letters,
They have been intercepted.
    Peregrine. Indeed, sir?
Best have a care.
    Sir Politic. Nay, so I will. [*Exit.*]
    Peregrine. This knight, 15
I may not lose him for my mirth, till night. [*Exit.*]

12 IT . . . BEST *"you were best to do so."*

Act II Scene iv

    [*Volpone's house. Volpone and Mosca.*]
Volpone. O, I am wounded!
    Mosca. Where, sir?
    Volpone. Not without;
Those blows were nothing, I could bear them ever.
But angry Cupid, bolting from her eyes,
Hath shot himself into me like a flame;
Where, now, he flings about his burning heat, 5
As in a furnace an ambitious fire

1 WITHOUT *outside, on the body.*
2 THOSE *blows given him by Corvino.*
3 BOLTING *springing, but also "shooting." A bolt is an arrow, and "Cupid's
   bolt" was a standard figure of speech.* HER *Celia's.*
6 AMBITIOUS *swelling.*

Whose vent is stopped. The fight is all within me.
I cannot live except thou help me, Mosca;
My liver melts, and I, without the hope
10 Of some soft air from her refreshing breath,
Am but a heap of cinders.

  Mosca.   'Las, good sir!
Would you had never seen her!

  Volpone.   Nay, would thou
Hadst never told me of her.

  Mosca.   Sir, 'tis true;
I do confess I was unfortunate,
15 And you unhappy; but I'm bound in conscience,
No less than duty, to effect my best
To your release of torment, and I will, sir.

  Volpone. Dear Mosca, shall I hope?

  Mosca.   Sir, more than dear,
I will not bid you to despair of aught
20 Within a human compass.

  Volpone.   O, there spoke
My better angel. Mosca, take my keys,
Gold, plate, and jewels, all's at thy devotion;
Employ them how thou wilt; nay, coin me too,
So thou in this but crown my longings—Mosca?
25 *Mosca.* Use but your patience.

  Volpone.   So I have.

---

9 LIVER *the supposed seat of violent passions such as love or hate.*
20 COMPASS *reach, possibility of achievement.*
22 DEVOTION *use.*
23 COIN *mint, turn to gold—but the word often had the meaning of counterfeiting.*
24 CROWN *satisfy, bring to fulfillment. A crown was also a coin.* —MOSCA? *a delay is indicated here; Mosca says nothing for a time until Volpone impatiently queries him.*

Mosca.   I doubt not   25
To bring success to your desires.
    Volpone.   Nay, then,
I not repent me of my late disguise.
    Mosca. If you can horn him, sir, you need not.
    Volpone.   True.
Besides, I never meant him for my heir.
Is not the color o' my beard and eyebrows   30
To make me known?
    Mosca.   No jot.
    Volpone.   I did it well.
    Mosca. So well, would I could follow you in mine,
With half the happiness; and, yet, I would
Escape your epilogue.
    Volpone.   But were they gulled
With a belief that I was Scoto?
    Mosca.   Sir,   35
Scoto himself could hardly have distinguished!
I have not time to flatter you now; we'll part,
And as I prosper, so applaud my art.   [*Exeunt.*]

27 NOT *do not.*
28 HORN *"give him a pair of horns,` i.e. cuckold him.*
30–1 IS . . . KNOWN *"Will not the distinctive color [red] . . . identify me?"*
31 NO JOT *not a bit.*
32 MINE *i.e. "my disguise and playing."*
34 YOUR EPILOGUE *your end, i.e. the beating. But Mosca's comment refers on*
    another level to the "epilogue" he plans to all Volpone's deception: bilking
    him of his fortune.
34 GULLED *fooled, taken in.*

Act II Scene v

[*Corvino's House.*]
[*Enter Corvino, Celia.*]

    Corvino. Death of mine honor, with the city's fool?
A juggling, tooth-drawing, prating mountebank?
And at a public window? where, whilst he,
With his strained action, and his dole of faces,
5 To his drug-lecture draws your itching ears,
A crew of old, unmarried, noted lechers
Stood leering up like satyrs: and you smile
Most graciously, and fan your favors forth,
To give your hot spectators satisfaction!
10 What, was your mountebank their call? their whistle?
Or were y' enamored on his copper rings?
His saffron jewel, with the toad stone in 't?
Or his embroiderèd suit, with the cope-stitch,
Made of a hearse cloth? or his old tilt-feather?
15 Or his starched beard! Well, you shall have him, yes.
He shall come home and minister unto you
The fricace for the mother. Or, let me see,

2 TOOTH-DRAWING *one of the major activities of itinerant quacks.*

3 PUBLIC *i.e. opening on the square.*

4 STRAINED ACTION *overdone theatrical gestures.* DOLE OF FACES *repertory of masks or facial expressions.*

7 SATYRS *mythological demi-gods noted for their cruelty and lechery.*

10 CALL *"a cry used to attract birds"* (OED).

11–15 COPPER RINGS . . . STARCHED BEARD *N.*

17 FRICACE . . . MOTHER *massage for an attack of hysteria—perhaps a standard medical treatment, but Corvino is also suggesting that Volpone will seduce Celia.*

I think you'd rather ~~mount?~~ would you not mount?
Why, if you'll mount, you may; yes truly, you may.
And so you may be seen, down to th' foot.   20
Get you a cittern, <u>Lady Vanity</u>, *(stock morality play char.)*
And be a <u>dealer</u> with the virtuous man; *prostitute with the*
Make one. I'll but protest myself a cuckold,   *virtuoso*
And save your dowry. I am a Dutchman, I!
For if you thought me an Italian,   25
You would be damned ere you did this, you whore!
Thou'dst tremble to imagine that the murder
Of father, mother, brother, all thy race,
Should follow as the subject of my justice.

   Celia. Good sir, have patience!
   Corvino.   What couldst thou propose   30
Less to thyself than in this heat of wrath,
And stung with my dishonor, I should strike [*Waves his sword.*]
~~This steel into thee, with as many stabs~~
As thou wert gazed upon with goatish eyes?

   Celia. Alas, sir, be appeased! I could not think   35
My being at the window should more now
Move your impatience than at other times.
   Corvino. No? not to seek and entertain a parley
With a known knave? before a multitude?

---

18 MOUNT *Corvino is again punning in an unpleasant manner. Celia, he suggests, may join the mountebank's troupe, mount the bank; and may also mount the mountebank.*

21 CITTERN *zither.* LADY VANITY *stock character in English morality plays.*

22 DEALER *prostitute.* VIRTUOUS MAN *pun on "*virtuoso*."*

23 MAKE ONE *"make a bargain."* PROTEST *declare.*

24 SAVE . . . DOWRY *N.*

24–5 DUTCHMAN . . . ITALIAN *by popular belief the Dutch were phlegmatic while the Italians were quick to anger and terrible in revenge.*

30–1 WHAT . . . THYSELF *"What less could you expect?"*

38 PARLEY *conversation.*

40 You were an actor with your handkerchief,
   Which he, most sweetly, kissed in the receipt.
   And might, no doubt, return it with a letter,
   And point the place where you might meet: your sister's,
   Your mother's, or your aunt's might serve the turn.

45   *Celia.* Why, dear sir, when do I make these excuses?
   Or ever stir abroad but to the church?
   And that so seldom—
     Corvino.   Well, it shall be less;
   And thy restraint before was liberty
   To what I now decree, and therefore mark me.

50 First, I will have this bawdy light dammed up;
   And till't be done, some two, or three yards off
   I'll chalk a line, o'er which if thou but chance
   To set thy desp'rate foot, more hell, more horror,
   More wild, remorseless rage shall seize on thee

55 Than on a conjurer that had heedless left
   His circle's safety ere his devil was laid.
   Then, here's a lock which I will hang upon thee,
   And, now I think on 't, I will keep thee backwards;
   Thy lodging shall be backwards, thy walks backwards,

60 Thy prospect—all be backwards, and no pleasure,
   That thou shalt know but backwards. Nay, since you force
   My honest nature, know it is your own
   Being too open makes me use you thus.

41 IN THE RECEIPT "*when he received it.*"
43 POINT *appoint.*
44 SERVE THE TURN "*do the trick.*"
46 ABROAD *out of doors.*
49 TO *compared to.* MARK *pay close attention to.*
53 DESP'RATE *reckless, violent.*
55-6 CONJURER . . . LAID *N.*
57 LOCK *chastity belt.*
60 PROSPECT *view.*

Since you will not contain your subtle nostrils
In a sweet room, but they must snuff the air   65
Of rank and sweaty passengers— *Knock within.*

                        One knocks.

Away, and be not seen, pain of thy life;
Not look toward the window; if thou dost— [*Celia starts to leave.*]
Nay, stay, hear this, let me not prosper, whore,
But I will make thee an anatomy,   70
Dissect thee mine own self, and read a lecture
Upon thee to the city, and in public.
Away! [*Exit Celia.*] Who's there? [*Enter servant.*]
   Servant.   'Tis Signior Mosca, sir.

64 SUBTLE *cunning (to smell out lust).*
65 AIR *odor.*
66 PASSENGERS *passersby.*
67 PAIN *on pain.*
68 NOT *do not.*
70 MAKE . . . ANATOMY *"anatomize you," i.e. describe your moral character detail by detail. So great is Corvino's fury, however, that he is also threatening literal dissection.*

Act II Scene vi

   Corvino. Let him come in, his master's dead. There's yet
Some good to help the bad.   [*Enter Mosca.*]
                     My Mosca, welcome!
I guess your news.
   Mosca.   I fear you cannot, sir.
   Corvino. Is't not his death?
   Mosca.   Rather the contrary.
   Corvino. Not his recovery?
   Mosca.   Yes, sir.
   Corvino.   I am cursed,   5

I am bewitched, my crosses meet to vex me.
How? how? how? how?

    Mosca.   Why, sir, with Scoto's oil!
Corbaccio and Voltore brought of it,
Whilst I was busy in an inner room—

10   *Corvino.* Death! that damned mountebank! but for the law,
Now, I could kill the rascal; 't cannot be
His oil should have that virtue. Ha' not I
Known him a common rogue, come fiddling in
To th' *osterìa*, with a tumbling whore,

15 And, when he has done all his forced tricks, been glad
Of a poor spoonful of dead wine, with flies in 't?
It cannot be. All his ingredients
Are a sheep's gall, a roasted bitch's marrow,
Some few sod earwigs, pounded caterpillars,

20 A little capon's grease, and fasting spittle;
I know 'em to a dram.

    Mosca.   I know not, sir;
But some on 't, there, they poured into his ears,
Some in his nostrils, and recovered him,
Applying but the fricace.

    Corvino.   Pox o' that fricace.

---

6 CROSSES *troubles.*

8 OF *"some of."*

14 OSTERÌA *inn. Scoto is now being described as an itinerant entertainer singing and performing for his supper.* TUMBLING WHORE *female acrobat and dancer.*

15 FORCED *strained, awkwardly apparent.*

17 IT *i.e. Volpone's recovery by means of the oil.*

19 SOD EARWIGS *boiled insects. The earwig was supposed to creep into the ear and the word came to have the figurative meaning of "flatterer."*

20 FASTING SPITTLE *fasting man's saliva; the implication being that Scoto is starving and poverty stricken.*

22 ON 'T *of it.* THERE *i.e. in Volpone's house.*

24 POX *the great pox, i.e. syphilis.*

Mosca. And since, to seem the more officious   25
And flatt'ring of his health, there they have had,
At extreme fees, the college of physicians
Consulting on him how they might restore him;
Where one would have a cataplasm of spices,
Another a flayed ape clapped to his breast,   30
A third would ha' it a dog, a fourth an oil
With wild cats' skins. At last, they all resolved
That to preserve him was no other means
But some young woman must be straight sought out,
Lusty, and full of juice, to sleep by him;   35
And to this service, most unhappily
And most unwillingly, am I now employed,
Which here I thought to pre-acquaint you with,
For your advice, since it concerns you most,
Because I would not do that thing might cross   40
Your ends, on whom I have my whole dependence, sir.
Yet, if I do it not they may delate
My slackness to my patron, work me out
Of his opinion; and there all your hopes,
Ventures, or whatsoever, are all frustrate.   45
I do but tell you, sir. Besides, they are all
Now striving who shall first present him. Therefore,

25 OFFICIOUS *dutiful.*
27 EXTREME FEES *enormous expense.*
29 CATAPLASM *large plaster.*
33 WAS *"there was."*
34 STRAIGHT *instantly.*
36 TO *on.*
41 ENDS *aims, intentions.*
42 DELATE *report.*
43–44 WORK . . . OPINION *"persuade him out of his high regard for me."*
45 FRUSTRATE *frustrated.*
46 I . . . SIR *"I only tell what may happen."*
47 PRESENT HIM *i.e. with the young woman prescribed.*

I could entreat you, briefly, conclude somewhat.
Prevent 'em if you can.

    Corvino.   Death to my hopes!
50 This is my villainous fortune! Best to hire
Some common courtesan?

    Mosca.   Ay, I thought on that, sir.
But they are all so subtle, full of art,
And age again doting and flexible,
So as—I cannot tell—we may perchance
55 Light on a quean may cheat us all.

    Corvino.   'Tis true.

    Mosca. No, no; it must be one that has no tricks, sir,
Some simple thing, a creature made unto it;
Some wench you may command. Ha' you no kinswoman?
God's so—Think, think, think, think, think, think, think, sir.
60 One o' the doctors offered there his daughter.

    Corvino. How!

    Mosca.   Yes, Signior Lupo, the physician.

    Corvino. His daughter!

    Mosca.   And a virgin, sir. Why, alas,
He knows the state of 's body, what it is;
That nought can warm his blood, sir, but a fever;
65 Nor any incantation raise his spirit;
A long forgetfulness hath seized that part.
Besides, sir, who shall know it? Some one or two—

48 BRIEFLY *quickly.* CONCLUDE SOMEWHAT *decide something, form some plan.*
49 PREVENT *in both the sense of "stop" and the literal meaning of "come before" or "anticipate."*
52 SUBTLE *cunning, tricky.* ART *wiles.*
53 AGE AGAIN *"old age on the other hand."* FLEXIBLE *pliable, gullible.*
55 QUEAN *whore.*
57 MADE UNTO *forced to, directed.*
59 SO *soul(?) Also a corruption of Italian,* cazzo, *the male organ.*
61 LUPO *wolf.*

Corvino. I pray thee give me leave.   *[Walks up and down*
and talks to himself.]

                        If any man
But I had had this luck—The thing in 't self,
I know, is nothing—Wherefore should not I   70
As well command my blood and my affections
As this dull doctor? In the point of honor
The cases are all one of wife and daughter.
   Mosca. [Aside.] I hear him coming.
   Corvino.   She shall do 't. 'Tis done.
'Slight, if this doctor, who is not engaged,   75
Unless 't be for his counsel, which is nothing,
Offer his daughter, what should I that am
So deeply in? I will prevent him; Wretch!
Covetous wretch! Mosca, I have determined.
   Mosca. How, sir?
   Corvino.   We'll make all sure. The party you wot of   80
Shall be <u>mine own wife, Mosca.</u>
   Mosca.   Sir, the thing
But that I would not seem to counsel you,
I should have motioned to you at the first.
And make your count, you have cut all their throats.

68 GIVE ME LEAVE *"excuse me."*
71 BLOOD *spirit.* AFFECTIONS *feelings.*
72 POINT *matter.*
73 CASES . . . OF *"it is the same with."*
74 COMING *"coming round," taking the bait.*
75 'SLIGHT *God's light.* ENGAGED *deeply involved.*
79 DETERMINED *decided.*
80 WOT *know.*
81 THE THING *"the very thing."*
83 MOTIONED *suggested.*
84 MAKE YOUR COUNT *"inventory Volpone's goods which you are sure to get"(?)*

85 Why, 'tis directly taking a possession!
And in his next fit, we may let him go.
'Tis but to pull the pillow from his head,
And he is throttled; 't had been done before
But for your scrupulous doubts.

    Corvino.   Ay, a plague on 't,
90 My conscience fools my wit! Well, I'll be brief,
And so be thou, lest they should be before us.
Go home, prepare him, tell him with what zeal
And willingness I do it; swear it was
On the first hearing, as thou mayst do, truly,
95 Mine own free motion.

    Mosca.   Sir, I warrant you,
I'll so possess him with it that the rest
Of his starved clients shall be banished all;
And only you received. But come not, sir,
Until I send, for I have something else
100 To ripen for your good, you must not know 't.

    Corvino. But do not you forget to send now.

    Mosca.   Fear not.

                                     [*Exit Mosca.*]

---

85 POSSESSION *in law* "*the detention or enjoyment of a thing by a person himself or another in his name*" (OED).

87 'TIS BUT "*We need only.*" FROM *from under.*

89 SCRUPULOUS *overly nice.*

90 WIT *reason.* BRIEF *quick.*

91 BEFORE *ahead of.*

95 FREE MOTION *unprompted proposal.*

Act II Scene vii

Corvino. Where are you, wife? My Celia? wife?
        [*Enter Celia crying.*]
                         What, blubbering?
Come, dry those tears. I think thou thought'st me in earnest?
Ha? by this light I talked so but to try thee.
Methinks the lightness of the occasion
Should ha' confirmed thee. Come, I am not jealous.   5
    Celia. No?
    Corvino.   Faith I am not, I, nor never was;
It is a poor unprofitable humor.
Do not I know if women have a will
They'll do 'gainst all the watches o' the world?
And that the fiercest spies are tamed with gold?   10
Tut, I am confident in thee, thou shalt see 't;
And see I'll give thee cause too, to believe it.
Come, kiss me. Go, and make thee ready straight
In all thy best attire, thy choicest jewels,
Put 'em all on, and, with 'em, thy best looks.   15
We are invited to a solemn feast
At old Volpone's, where it shall appear
How far I am free from jealousy or fear.   [*Exeunt.*]

3 TRY *test.*
4 LIGHTNESS *triviality.* OCCASION *i.e. leaning out the window, dropping hand-kerchief.*
5 CONFIRMED *reassured.*
6 FAITH "*in faith.*"
8 WILL *sexual appetite.*
9 'GAINST *despite.* WATCHES *precautions.*
10 TAMED *bribed.*
16 SOLEMN FEAST *formal banquet.*

Act III Scene i

[handwritten: Mosca's soliloq.]

[handwritten: a parasite is a most precious thing]

[*A street. Mosca alone.*]
   Mosca. I fear I shall begin to grow in love
With my dear self and my most prosp'rous parts,
They do so spring and burgeon; I can feel
A whimsy i' my blood. I know not how,
5 Success hath made me wanton. I could skip
Out of my skin, now, like a subtle snake,
I am so limber. O! your parasite
Is a most precious thing, dropped from above,
Not bred 'mongst clods and clodpolls, here on earth.
10 I muse the mystery was not made a science,
   It is so liberally professed! Almost
   All the wise world is little else in nature
   But parasites or sub-parasites. And yet,
   I mean not those that have your bare town-art,
15 To know who's fit to feed 'em; have no house,

   2 PROSP'ROUS PARTS *flourishing talents.*
   4 WHIMSY *dizziness, whirling.*
   5 WANTON *playful.*
   6 SUBTLE *cunning; also dexterous, elusive.*
   9 CLODPOLLS *dolts.*
   10 MYSTERY *craft.* SCIENCE *N.*
   11 LIBERALLY PROFESSED *freely practiced. See N. to line 10.*
   14 BARE TOWN-ART *i.e. crude skill.*

No family, no care, and therefore mold
Tales for men's ears, to bait that sense; or get
Kitchen-invention, and some stale receipts
To please the belly, and the groin; nor those,
With their court-dog-tricks, that can fawn and fleer,   20
Make their revènue out of legs and faces,
Echo my lord, and lick away a moth.
But your fine, elegant rascal, that can rise
And stoop, almost together, like an arrow;
Shoot through the air as nimbly as a star;
Turn short as doth a swallow; and be here,
And there, and here, and yonder, all at once;
Present to any humor, all occasion;
And change a visor swifter than a thought.
This is the creature had the art born with him;   30
Toils not to learn it, but doth practice it
Out of most excellent nature: and such sparks
Are the true parasites, others but their zanies.

16–17 MOLD TALES *invent gossip and slander.*
18 KITCHEN-INVENTION *recipes for elaborate dishes.* RECEIPTS *recipes.*
19 GROIN *N.*
20 FLEER *smile obsequiously.*
21 REVÈNUE *accented on second syllable.* LEGS AND FACES *bows and smirks.*
22 LICK . . . MOTH *N.*
28 PRESENT . . . OCCASION *"ready to satisfy any whim and meet any situation."*
29 VISOR *mask, i.e. personality.*
33 ZANIES *clowns, assistants—see II.2, where Nano plays Scoto's zany.*

Act III Scene ii

[*Enter Bonario.*]

Mosca. Who's this? Bonario? Old Corbaccio's son?
The person I was bound to seek. Fair sir,
You are happ'ly met.

Bonario.　　　　　That cannot be by thee.

Mosca. Why, sir?

Bonario.　　　　　Nay, 'pray thee know thy way and leave me:
5 I would be loth to interchange discourse
With such a mate as thou art.

Mosca.　　　　　Courteous sir,
Scorn not my poverty.

Bonario.　　　　　Not I, by heaven;
But thou shalt give me leave to hate thy baseness.

Mosca. Baseness?

Bonario.　　　　　Ay, answer me, is not thy sloth
10 Sufficient argument? thy flattery?
Thy means of feeding?

Mosca.　　　　　Heaven be good to me!
These imputations are too common, sir,
And eas'ly stuck on virtue when she's poor.
You are unequal to me, and howe'er
15 Your sentence may be righteous, yet you are not,
That ere you know me, thus proceed in censure.
St. Mark bear witness 'gainst you, 'tis inhuman. [*He cries.*]

2 BOUND *on my way.*
6 MATE *low person.*
10 ARGUMENT *reason.*
14 UNEQUAL *unjust.* HOWE'ER *no matter how much.*

104

Bonario. [*Aside.*] What? does he weep? the sign is soft and good.
I do repent me that I was so harsh.

Mosca. 'Tis true that swayed by strong necessity,   20
I am enforced to eat my carefull bread
With too much obsequy; 'tis true, beside,
That I am fain to spin mine own poor raiment
Out of my mere observance, being not born
To a free fortune; but that I have done   25
Base offices, in rending friends asunder,
Dividing families, betraying counsels,
Whispering false lies, or mining men with praises,
Trained their credulity with perjuries,
Corrupted chastity, or am in love   30
With mine own tender ease, but would not rather
Prove the most rugged and laborious course,
That might redeem my present estimation,
Let me here perish, in all hope of goodness.

Bonario. [*Aside.*]—This cannot be a personated passion—   35
I was to blame, so to mistake thy nature;
Pray thee forgive me and speak out thy business.

Mosca. Sir, it concerns you, and though I may seem
At first to make a main offence in manners,
And in my gratitude unto my master,   40
Yet, for the pure love which I bear all right,

20 SWAYED *controlled.*
21 CAREFULL *full of care, i.e. gotten with pain.*
22 OBSEQUY *humility.*
23 FAIN *obliged.* SPIN . . . RAIMENT *get clothing.*
24 MERE OBSERVANCE *service alone.*
28 MINING *undermining.*
32 PROVE *endure.*
33 ESTIMATION *reputation.*
35 PERSONATED *pretended.* PASSION *strong feeling.*
39 MAIN *great.*

And hatred of the wrong, I must reveal it.
This very hour your father is in purpose
To disinherit you—
    Bonario.   How!
    Mosca.   And thrust you forth
45 As a mere stranger to his blood; 'tis true, sir.
The work no way engageth me, but as
I claim an interest in the general state
Of goodness and true virtue, which I hear
T' abound in you, and for which mere respect,
50 Without a second aim, sir, I have done it.
    Bonario. This tale hath lost thee much of the late trust
Thou hadst with me; it is impossible.
I know not how to lend it any thought
My father should be so unnatural.
55   *Mosca.* It is a confidence that well becomes
Your piety, and formed, no doubt, it is
From your own simple innocence, which makes
Your wrong more monstrous and abhorred. But, sir,
I now will tell you more. This very minute
60 It is, or will be doing; and if you
Shall be but pleased to go with me, I'll bring you,
I dare not say where you shall see, but where
Your ear shall be a witness of the deed;
Hear yourself written bastard and professed
65 The common issue of the earth.

    45 MERE *complete.*
    49 FOR . . . RESPECT *only for this reason.*
    50 SECOND AIM *concealed purpose.*
    53 LEND . . . THOUGHT *believe it at all.*
    56 PIETY *filial love* (*Latin,* pietas).
    64 PROFESSED *proclaimed.*
    65 COMMON . . . EARTH *a man without family or position.*

Bonario.   I'm mazed!   65

Mosca. Sir, if I do it not, draw your just sword
And score your vengeance on my front and face;
Mark me your villain. You have too much wrong,
And I do suffer for you, sir. My heart
Weeps blood in anguish—

Bonario.   Lead, I follow thee.   [*Exeunt.*]   70

65 MAZED *bewildered, confused.*
67 SCORE *mark.* FRONT *forehead.*

Act III Scene iii

[*Volpone's house.*]

Volpone. Mosca stays long, methinks. Bring forth your sports
And help to make the wretched time more sweet.

[*Enter Nano, Castrone, Androgyno.*]

Nano. Dwarf, fool, and eunuch, well met here we be.
A question it were now, whether of us three,
Being, all, the known delicates of a rich man,   5
In pleasing him, claim the precedency can?

Castrone. I claim for myself.

Androgyno.   And so doth the fool.

Nano. 'Tis foolish indeed, let me set you both to school.
First for your dwarf, he's little and witty,
And everything, as it is little, is pretty;   10
Else, why do men say to a creature of my shape,
So soon as they see him, "It's a pretty little ape"?

4 WHETHER *which.*
5 KNOWN DELICATES *acknowledged favourites.*
8 SET . . . TO SCHOOL *instruct.*
10 AS *to the degree that.*

And, why a pretty ape? but for pleasing imitation
Of greater men's action, in a ridiculous fashion.
15 Beside, this feat body of mine doth not crave
Half the meat, drink, and cloth one of your bulks will have.
Admit your fool's face be the mother of laughter,
Yet, for his brain, it must always come after;
And though that do feed him, it's a pitiful case
20 His body is beholding to such a bad face.   *One knocks.*
    Volpone. Who's there? My couch, away, look, Nano, see;
Give me my caps first—go, inquire.

                                    [*Exeunt Castrone, Androgyno.*]
                                    [*Volpone lies down in his bed.*]
                                    Now Cupid

Send it be Mosca, and with fair return.
    Nano. It is the beauteous madam—
    Volpone.   Wouldbe—is it?
25 *Nano.* The same.
    Volpone.   Now, torment on me; squire her in,
For she will enter, or dwell here forever.
Nay, quickly, that my fit were past. I fear   [*Exit Nano.*]
A second hell too: that my loathing this
Will quite expel my appetite to the other.
30 Would she were taking, now, her tedious leave.
Lord, how it threats me, what I am to suffer!

15 FEAT *elegant.*
18 COME AFTER *follow, i.e. be second, less important.*
19 THAT *i.e. the face, the mouth.*
23 FAIR RETURN *good luck—the phrase has commercial suggestions: a "fair re-*
    turn" on a venture.
28 THIS *i.e. Lady Wouldbe.*
29 OTHER *i.e. Celia.*

Act III Scene iv

[*Enter Nano with Lady Wouldbe.*]

  Lady Wouldbe. [*To Nano.*] I thank you, good sir. Pray you signify

Unto your patron I am here—This band

Shows not my neck enough.—I trouble you, sir;

Let me request you bid one of my women

Come hither to me. In good faith, I am dressed   5

Most favourably today! It is no matter;

'Tis well enough. [*Enter 1st Woman.*] Look, see these petulant things!

How they have done this!

  Volpone. [*Aside.*]   —I do feel the fever

Ent'ring in at mine ears. O for a charm

To fright it hence—

  Lady Wouldbe.   Come nearer. Is this curl   10

In his right place? or this? Why is this higher

Than all the rest? You ha' not washed your eyes yet?

Or do they not stand even i' your head?

Where's your fellow? Call her.   [*Exit 1st Woman.*]

  Nano. [*Aside.*]   Now, St. Mark

Deliver us! Anon she'll beat her women   15

Because her nose is red. [*Re-enter 1st Woman with 2nd Woman.*]

  Lady Wouldbe.   I pray you, view

This tire, forsooth; are all things apt, or no?

2 BAND *ruff.*
5–6 I . . . FAVORABLY *ironic.*
12–13 YOU . . . HEAD "*Can't you see straight?*"
17 TIRE *hair arrangement.*

1st Woman. One hair a little, here, sticks out, forsooth.

Lady Wouldbe. Dost so, forsooth? And where was your dear
sight

20 When it did so, forsooth? What now! Bird-eyed?
And you too? Pray you both approach and mend it.
Now, by that light, I muse you're not ashamed!
I, that have preached these things, so oft, unto you,
Read you the principles, argued all the grounds,

25 Disputed every fitness, every grace,
Called you to counsel of so frequent dressings—

Nano. [*Aside.*] More carefully than of your fame or honor.

Lady Wouldbe. Made you acquainted what an ample dowry
The knowledge of these things would be unto you,

30 Able, alone, to get you noble husbands
At your return; and you, thus, to neglect it!
Besides, you seeing what a curious nation
Th' Italians are, what will they say of me?
"The English lady cannot dress herself."

35 Here's a fine imputation to our country!
Well, go your ways, and stay i' the next room.
This fucus was too coarse, too; it's no matter.
Good sir, you'll give 'em entertainment?

[*Exit Nano with Women.*]

Volpone. The storm comes toward me.

Lady Wouldbe.   How does my Volp?

20 BIRD-EYED *frightened(?)*
24 GROUNDS *fundamentals—dressing is treated here like a science or the art of
government.*
27 FAME *reputation.*
31 RETURN *i.e. to England.*
32 CURIOUS *particular in small details.*
37 FUCUS *cosmetic for covering up complexion, "pancake makeup."*
38 GIVE 'EM ENTERTAINMENT *look out for them.*

Volpone. Troubled with noise, I cannot sleep; I dreamt   40
That a strange fury entered, now, my house,
And, with the dreadful tempest of her breath,
Did cleave my roof asunder.

Lady Wouldbe.   Believe me, and I
Had the most *fearful* dream, could I remember 't—

Volpone. [*Aside.*] Out on my fate! I ha' giv'n her the occasion   45
How to torment me. She will tell me hers.

Lady Wouldbe. Methought the golden mediocrity,   *(see note p 219*
Polite, and delicate—

Volpone.   Oh, if you do love me,
No more; I sweat, and suffer, at the mention
Of *any* dream; feel how I tremble yet.   50

                              [*Placing her hand on his heart.*]

Lady Wouldbe. Alas, good soul! the passion of the heart,
Seed-pearl were good now, boiled with syrup of apples,
Tincture of gold, and coral, citron-pills,
Your elecampane root, myrobalanes—

Volpone. [*Aside.*] Ay me, I have ta'en a grasshopper by the
      wing!   55

Lady Wouldbe. Burnt silk and amber. You have muscadel
Good in the house—

Volpone.   You will not drink and part?

Lady Wouldbe. No, fear not that. I doubt we shall not get
Some English saffron, half a dram would serve,
Your sixteen cloves, a little musk, dried mints,   60
Bugloss, and barley-meal—

45 OCCASION *means and opportunity.*
47 GOLDEN MEDIOCRITY *N.*
51 PASSION OF THE HEART *stomach gas pressing on the heart.*
52–6 SEED-PEARL . . . MUSCADEL *a catalogue of popular remedies.*
55 GRASSHOPPER *referring to constant whirring noise made by captive grass-*
      hoppers.
58 DOUBT *fear.*

Volpone.   [*Aside.*] She's in again.
Before I feigned diseases, now I have one.
   Lady Wouldbe. And these applied with a right scarlet cloth.
   Volpone. [*Aside.*] Another flood of words! a very torrent!
65   *Lady Wouldbe.* Shall I, sir, make you a poultice?
   Volpone.   No, no, no.
I'm very well, you need prescribe no more.
   Lady Wouldbe. I have, a little, studied physic; but now
I'm all for music, save, i' the forenoons
An hour or two for painting. I would have
70 A lady, indeed, to have all letters and arts,
Be able to discourse, to write, to paint,
But principal, as Plato holds, your music,
And so does wise Pythagoras, I take it,
Is your true rapture, when there is concent
75 In face, in voice, and clothes, and is, indeed,
Our sex's chiefest ornament.
   Volpone.   The poet
As old in time as Plato, and as knowing,
Says that your highest female grace is silence.
   Lady Wouldbe. Which o' your poets? Petrarch? or Tasso? or
      Dante?
80 Guarini? Ariosto? Aretine?
Cieco di Hadria? I have read them all.
   Volpone. [*Aside.*] Is everything a cause to my destruction?
   Lady Wouldbe. I think I ha' two or three of 'em about me.
   Volpone. [*Aside.*] The sun, the sea, will sooner both stand still
85 Than her eternal tongue! Nothing can scape it.

   63 RIGHT *true.*
   67 PHYSIC *medicine.*
   74 CONCENT *agreement, harmony.*
   76 POET *Sophocles,* Ajax *293.*
   80-1 ARETINE? CIECO DI HADRIA? *N.*

Lady Wouldbe. Here's *Pastor Fido*—   [*Producing a book.*]
Volpone.   [*Aside.*] Profess obstinate silence;
That's now my safest.
  Lady Wouldbe.   All our English writers,
I mean such as are happy in th' Italian,
Will deign to steal out of this author, mainly;
Almost as much as from Montagniè.   90
He has so modern and facile a vein,
Fitting the time, and catching the court-ear.
Your Petrarch is more passionate, yet he,
In days of sonneting, trusted 'em with much.
Dante is hard, and few can understand him.   95
But for a desperate wit, there's Aretine!
Only, his pictures are a little obscene—
You mark me not.
  Volpone.   Alas, my mind's perturbed.
  Lady Wouldbe. Why, in such cases, we must cure ourselves,
Make use of our philosophy—
  Volpone.   O'y me!   100
  Lady Wouldbe. And as we find our passions do rebel,
Encounter 'em with reason, or divert 'em
By giving scope unto some other humor
Of lesser danger: as, in politic bodies

86 PASTOR FIDO The Faithful Shepherd (*1590*), *Guarini's pastoral play.*
88 HAPPY *fluent.*
90 MONTAGNIÈ *Montaigne, the French essayist. Pronounced with four syllables here.*
92 COURT-EAR *ear of courtiers.*
93-4 PETRARCH . . . MUCH *N.*
96 DESPERATE *outrageous.*
97 PICTURES *Aretino wrote poems to accompany a series of obscene drawings.*
102 ENCOUNTER *battle.*
103 SCOPE *free play.* HUMOR *desire.*
104 POLITIC BODIES *kingdoms.*

105 There's nothing more doth overwhelm the judgment,
And clouds the understanding, than too much
Settling and fixing, and, as 'twere, subsiding
Upon one object. For the incorporating
Of these same outward things into that part
110 Which we call mental, leaves some certain feces
That stop the organs, and, as Plato says,
Assassinates our knowledge.
    Volpone.   [*Aside.*] Now, the spirit
Of patience help me!
    Lady Wouldbe.   Come, in faith, I must
Visit you more adays and make you well;
115 Laugh and be lusty.
    Volpone. [*Aside.*] My good angel save me!
    Lady Wouldbe. There was but one sole man in all the world
With whom I e'er could sympathize; and he
Would lie you often, three, four hours together
To hear me speak, and be sometime so rapt,
120 As he would answer me quite from the purpose,
Like you, and you are like him, just. I'll discourse,
An 't be but only, sir, to bring you asleep,
How we did spend our time and loves together,
For some six years.
    Volpone.   Oh, oh, oh, oh, oh, oh.
125   *Lady Wouldbe.* For we were *coaetanei*, and brought up—
    Volpone. Some power, some fate, some fortune rescue me!

109 OUTWARD THINGS *the object on which the mind has fixed, N.*
118 LIE YOU *lie.*
120 FROM THE PURPOSE *nothing to the point.*
125 COAETANEI *of the same age.*

Act III Scene v

[*Enter Mosca.*]

Mosca. God save you, madam!

Lady Wouldbe.   Good sir.

Volpone.   Mosca, welcome!

Welcome to my redemption.

Mosca.   Why, sir?

Volpone.   Oh,

Rid me of this my torture quickly, there,

My madam with the everlasting voice;

The bells in time of pestilence ne'er made   5

Like noise, or were in that perpetual motion!

The cock-pit comes not near it. All my house,

But now, steamed like a bath with her thick breath.

A lawyer could not have been heard; nor scarce

Another woman, such a hail of words   10

She has let fall. For hell's sake, rid her hence.

Mosca. Has she presented?

Volpone.   Oh, I do not care;

I'll take her absence upon any price,

With any loss.

Mosca.   Madam—

Lady Wouldbe.   I ha' brought your patron

A toy, a cap here, of mine own work.

---

5 BELLS . . . PESTILENCE *the bells in London rang almost without ceasing during times of the plague.*

7 COCK-PIT *where cock fights were put on.*

12 PRESENTED *given a present.*

    Mosca.   'Tis well.
I had forgot to tell you I saw your knight
Where you'd little think it.
    Lady Wouldbe.   Where?
    Mosca.   Marry,
Where yet, if you make haste, you may apprehend him,
Rowing upon the water in a gondole,
20 With the most cunning courtesan of Venice.
    Lady Wouldbe. Is't true?
    Mosca.   Pursue 'em, and believe your eyes.
Leave me to make your gift. [*Exit Lady Wouldbe.*] I knew 'twould
    take.
For lightly, they that use themselves most license,
Are still most jealous.
    Volpone.   Mosca, hearty thanks
25 For thy quick fiction and delivery of me.
Now to my hopes, what sayst thou? [*Re-enter Lady Wouldbe.*]
    Lady Wouldbe.   But do you hear, sir?
    Volpone. Again! I fear a paroxysm.
    Lady Wouldbe.   Which way
Rowed they together?
    Mosca.   Toward the Rialto.
    Lady Wouldbe. I pray you lend me your dwarf.
    Mosca.   I pray you, take him.
                        [*Exit Lady Wouldbe.*]
30 Your hopes, sir, are like happy blossoms: fair,
And promise timely fruit, if you will stay
But the maturing; keep you at your couch.
Corbaccio will arrive straight with the will;
When he is gone, I'll tell you more.   [*Exit Mosca.*]
    Volpone.   My blood,

23 LIGHTLY *commonly.* USE . . . LICENSE *are most free (morally).*
24 STILL *always.*

My spirits are returned; I am alive;   35
And, like your wanton gamester at primero,
Whose thought had whispered to him, not go less,
Methinks I lie, and draw—for an encounter.

> [*He draws the curtains across his bed.*]

36 WANTON GAMESTER *reckless gambler.*
36 PRIMERO *N.*

Act III Scene vi

> [*Mosca leads Bonario on stage and hides him.*]

Mosca. Sir, here concealed you may hear all. But pray you

> *One knocks.*

Have patience, sir; the same's your father knocks.
I am compelled to leave you.
    Bonario.   Do so. Yet
Cannot my thought imagine this a truth.

Act III Scene vii

> [*Mosca opens door and admits Corvino and Celia.*]

Mosca. Death on me! you are come too soon, what meant you?
Did not I say I would send?
    Corvino.   Yes, but I feared
You might forget it, and then they prevent us.
    Mosca. Prevent! [*Aside.*] —Did e'er man haste so for his horns?

2 SEND *send word when to come.*
3 THEY *i.e. the other legacy hunters.*
4 HORNS *the symbol of the cuckold.*

5 A courtier would not ply it so for a place.—
 Well, now there's no helping it, stay here;
 I'll presently return. [*He moves to one side.*]
  Corvino.   Where are you, Celia?
 You know not wherefore I have brought you hither?
  Celia. Not well, except you told me.
  Corvino.   Now I will:
10 Hark hither. [*He leads her aside and whispers to her.*]
  Mosca. *To Bonario.* Sir, your father hath sent word,
 It will be half an hour ere he come;
 And therefore, if you please to walk the while
 Into that gallery—at the upper end
 There are some books to entertain the time.
15 And I'll take care no man shall come unto you, sir.
  Bonario. Yes, I will stay there. [*Aside.*] I do doubt this fellow.
       [*Exit.*]

  Mosca. There, he is far enough; he can hear nothing.
 And for his father, I can keep him off.   [*Returns to Volpone's*
  Corvino. Nay, now, there is no starting back, and   *couch, opens*
   therefore   *the curtains,*
20 Resolve upon it: I have so decreed.   *and whispers*
 It must be done. Nor would I move 't afore,   *to him.*]
 Because I would avoid all shifts and tricks,
 That might deny me.
  Celia.   Sir, let me beseech you,
 Affect not these strange trials; if you doubt

---

5 PLY . . . PLACE *work so hard for an office at court.*

7 PRESENTLY *immediately.*

9 EXCEPT *except what.*

14 ENTERTAIN *pass.*

21 MOVE *suggest.*

22 SHIFTS *evasions.*

24 AFFECT . . . TRIALS *"do not pretend to make such unusual tests"* (of her virtue).

My chastity, why, lock me up forever;   25
Make me the heir of darkness. Let me live
Where I may please your fears, if not your trust.
   Corvino. Believe it, I have no such humor, I.
All that I speak I mean; yet I am not mad;
Not horn-mad, see you? Go to, show yourself   30
Obedient, and a wife.
   Celia.   O heaven!
   Corvino.   I say it,
Do so.
   Celia. Was this the train?
   Corvino.   I've told you reasons:
What the physicians have set down; how much
It may concern me; what my engagements are;
My means, and the necessity of those means   35
For my recovery; wherefore, if you be
Loyal and mine, be won, respect my venture.
   Celia. Before your honor?
   Corvino.   Honor! tut, a breath.
There's no such thing in nature; a mere term
Invented to awe fools. What, is my gold   40
The worse for touching? clothes for being looked on?
Why, this's no more. An old, decrepit wretch,
That has no sense, no sinew; takes his meat
With others' fingers; only knows to gape
When you do scald his gums; a voice, a shadow;   45
And what can this man hurt you?

30 HORN-MAD *with fear of being a cuckold.*
32 TRAIN *trap.*
34 ENGAGEMENTS *financial commitments.*
35 MEANS *i.e. becoming Volpone's heir.*
36 RECOVERY *regaining financial stability.*
37 VENTURE *commercial enterprise.*
43 SENSE *sensory perception.*

Celia.   Lord, what spirit
Is this hath entered him?
    Corvino.   And for your fame,
That's such a jig; as if I would go tell it,
Cry it, on the Piazza! Who shall know it
50 But he that cannot speak it, and this fellow,
Whose lips are i' my pocket, save yourself.
—If you'll proclaim 't, you may—I know no other
Should come to know it.
    Celia.   Are heaven and saints then nothing?
Will they be blind, or stupid?
    Corvino.   How?
    Celia.   Good sir,
55 Be jealous still, emulate them, and think
What hate they burn with toward every sin.
    Corvino. I grant you. If I thought it were a sin
I would not urge you. Should I offer this
To some young Frenchman, or hot Tuscan blood
60 That had read Aretine, conned all his prints,
Knew every quirk within lust's labyrinth,
And were professed critic in lechery;
And I would look upon him, and applaud him,
This were a sin; but here, 'tis contrary,
65 A pious work, mere charity, for physic
And honest policy to assure mine own.
    Celia. O heaven! canst thou suffer such a change?

47 FAME *reputation.*
48 JIG *farce.*
51 LIPS . . . POCKET *Mosca will not speak because Corvino owns him.*
57 I GRANT YOU *"Agreed."*
60 PRINTS *the obscene pictures referred to above.*
62 PROFESSED CRITIC *connoisseur.*
63 AND *if.*
66 OWN *i.e. inheritance.*

Volpone. Thou art mine honor, Mosca, and my pride,
My joy, my tickling, my delight! Go, bring 'em.
    Mosca. Please you draw near, sir.
    Corvino.   Come on, what—   70
                                        [*She hangs back.*]
You will not be rebellious? By that light—
                             [*He drags her to the bed.*]
    Mosca. [*To Volpone.*] Sir, Signior Corvino, here, is come to see
    you.
    Volpone. Oh!
    Mosca.   And hearing of the consultation had,
So lately, for your health, is come to offer,
Or rather, sir, to prostitute—
    Corvino.   Thanks, sweet Mosca.   75
    Mosca. Freely, unasked, or unentreated—
    Corvino.   Well.
    Mosca. As the true, fervent instance of his love,
His own most fair and proper wife, the beauty
Only of price in Venice—
    Corvino.   'Tis well urged.
    Mosca. To be your comfortress, and to preserve you.   80
    Volpone. Alas, I'm past already! Pray you, thank him
For his good care and promptness; but for that,
'Tis a vain labor e'en to fight 'gainst heaven;
Applying fire to a stone, uh, uh, uh, uh!
Making a dead leaf grow again. I take   85
His wishes gently, though; and you may tell him
What I've done for him. Marry, my state is hopeless!
Will him to pray for me, and t' use his fortune
With reverence when he comes to't.

79 ONLY OF PRICE *uniquely beautiful.*
84 APPLYING . . . STONE *proverbial statement of absolute futility.*

     Mosca.   Do you hear, sir?

90 Go to him with your wife.

     Corvino. [*To Celia.*]   Heart of my father!

Wilt thou persist thus? Come, I pray thee, come.

Thou seest 'tis nothing, Celia. By this hand   [*Raising his hand.*]

I shall grow violent. Come, do 't, I say.

     Celia. Sir, kill me rather. I will take down poison,

95 Eat burning coals, do anything—

     Corvino.   Be damned!

Heart! I will drag thee hence home by the hair,

Cry thee a strumpet through the streets, rip up

Thy mouth unto thine ears, and slit thy nose,

Like a raw rotchet!—Do not tempt me, come.

100 Yield, I am loth—Death! I will buy some slave

Whom I will kill, and bind thee to him, alive;

And at my window hang you forth, devising

Some monstrous crime, which I, in capital letters,

Will eat into thy flesh with aquafortis,

105 And burning cor'sives, on this stubborn breast.

Now, by the blood thou hast incensed, I'll do 't!

     Celia. Sir, what you please, you may; I am your martyr.

     Corvino. Be not thus obstinate, I ha' not deserved it.

Think who it is entreats you. Pray thee, sweet;

110 Good faith, thou shalt have jewels, gowns, attires,

What thou wilt, think and ask. Do, but go kiss him.

Or touch him, but. For my sake. At my suit.

This once. [*She refuses.*] No? Not? I shall remember this.

Will you disgrace me thus? D' you thirst my undoing?

---

95 EAT BURNING COALS *method of suicide used by Portia, Brutus' wife.*

99 ROTCHET *a variety of fish.*

104 AQUAFORTIS *acid.*

105 COR'SIVES *corrosives.*

Mosca. Nay, gentle lady, be advised.

Corvino.   . No, no.   115
She has watched her time. God's precious, this is scurvy,
'Tis very scurvy; and you are—
   Mosca.   Nay, good sir.
   Corvino. An errant locust, by heaven, a locust! Whore,
Crocodile, that hast thy tears prepared,
Expecting how thou'lt bid 'em flow.
   Mosca.   Nay, pray you, sir!   120
She will consider.
   Celia.   Would my life would serve
To satisfy.
   Corvino. 'Sdeath! if she would but speak to him,
And save my reputation, 'twere somewhat;
But spitefully to effect my utter ruin!
   Mosca. Ay, now you've put your fortune in her hands.   125
Why i' faith, it is her modesty, I must quit her.
If you were absent, she would be more coming;
I know it, and dare undertake for her.
What woman can before her husband? Pray you,
Let us depart and leave her here.
   Corvino.   Sweet Celia,   130
Thou may'st redeem all yet; I'll say no more.
If not, esteem yourself as lost.   [*She begins to leave with him.*]
                    Nay, stay there.
                         [*Exit Mosca and Corvino.*]

115 ADVISED *persuaded by the argument.*
116 WATCHED HER TIME *waited for her moment.*
118 ERRANT *either "far roving" or a form of "arrant."*
119 CROCODILE . . . TEARS *N.*
126 QUIT *excuse.*
127 COMING *agreeable.*
128 UNDERTAKE FOR *warrant.*

Act III Scene vii

    Celia. O God, and his good angels! whither, whither,
Is shame fled human breasts? that with such ease
135 Men dare put off your honors, and their own?
Is that, which ever was a cause of life,
Now placed beneath the basest circumstance,
And modesty an exile made, for money?
    Volpone. Ay, in Corvino, and such earth-fed minds,   *He leaps*
140 That never tasted the true heaven of love.   *off from*
Assure thee, Celia, he that would sell thee,   *the couch.*
Only for hope of gain, and that uncertain,
He would have sold his part of Paradise
For ready money, had he met a cope-man.
145 Why art thou mazed to see me thus revived?
Rather applaud thy beauty's miracle;
'Tis thy great work, that hath, not now alone,
But sundry times raised me in several shapes,
And, but this morning, like a mountebank,
150 To see thee at thy window. Ay, before
I would have left my practice for thy love,
In varying figures I would have contended
With the blue Proteus, or the hornèd flood.
Now, art thou welcome.
    Celia.   Sir!
    Volpone.   Nay, fly me not.
155 Nor let thy false imagination
That I was bed-rid, make thee think I am so:
Thou shalt not find it. I am, now, as fresh,

135 YOUR *i.e. God's and his angels'.*
137 CIRCUMSTANCE *matter of little importance.*
144 COPE-MAN *merchant.*
145 MAZED *amazed.*
151 PRACTICE *scheming.*
152 FIGURES *shapes, disguises.*
153 BLUE . . . FLOOD *N.*

124

As hot, as high, and in as jovial plight
As when in that so celebrated scene
At recitation of our comedy, 160
For entertainment of the great Valois,
I acted young <u>Antinous,</u> and attracted
The eyes and ears of all the ladies present,
T' admire each graceful gesture, note, and footing.

Song 165

Come, my Celia, let us prove,
While we can, the sports of love;
Time will not be ours forever,
He, at length, our good will sever;
Spend not then his gifts in vain. 170
Suns that set may rise again;
But if once we lose this light,
'Tis with us perpetual night.
Why should we defer our joys?
Fame and rumor are but toys. 175
Cannot we delude the eyes
Of a few poor household spies?
Or his easier ears beguile,
Thus removèd by our wile?
'Tis no sin love's fruits to steal, 180
But the sweet thefts to reveal:
To be taken, to be seen,
These have crimes accounted been.

158 JOVIAL PLIGHT *happy condition, but Jove and his love for earthly maidens is referred to.*
161 GREAT VALOIS *N.*
162 ANTINOUS *N.*
164 FOOTING *movement.*
165 SONG *N.*
166 PROVE *try, test.*
175 TOYS *trifles.*

Act III Scene vii

Celia.   Some serene blast me, or dire lightning strike
185   This my offending face.

   Volpone.   Why droops my Celia?
Thou hast in place of a base husband found
A worthy lover; use thy fortune well,
With secrecy and pleasure. See, behold,

                                    [*Pointing to his treasure.*]

What thou art queen of; not in expectation,
190   As I feed others, but possessed and crowned.
See, here, a rope of pearl, and each more orient
Than that the brave Egyptian queen caroused;
Dissolve and drink 'em. See, a carbuncle
May put out both the eyes of our St. Mark;
195   A diamond would have bought Lollia Paulina
When she came in like star-light, hid with jewels
That were the spoils of provinces; take these,
And wear, and lose 'em; yet remains an earring
To purchase them again, and this whole state.
200   A gem but worth a private patrimony
Is nothing; we will eat such at a meal.
The heads of parrots, tongues of nightingales,
The brains of peacocks, and of estriches
Shall be our food, and, could we get the phoenix,

184   SERENE *poisonous mist.*
185   OFFENDING *i.e. because its beauty attracts Volpone.*
191   ORIENT *precious.*
192   EGYPTIAN QUEEN *Cleopatra, who at an extravagant banquet drank pearls dissolved in vinegar.* CAROUSED *drank.*
193   CARBUNCLE *rounded red gem, e.g. a ruby.*
194   MAY . . . ST. MARK *N.*
195   LOLLIA PAULINA *wife of a Roman governor of a province who covered herself with jewels taken from the province.*
200   PRIVATE PATRIMONY *single inheritance.*
204   PHOENIX *mythical bird. Only one was believed to exist at a time, and from his ashes another was born.*

126

Though nature lost her kind, she were our dish.   205

   Celia. Good sir, these things might move a mind affected
With such delights; but I, whose innocence
Is all I can think wealthy, or worth th' enjoying,
And which, once lost, I have nought to lose beyond it,
Cannot be taken with these sensual baits.   210
If you have conscience—

   Volpone.   'Tis the beggar's virtue;
If thou hast wisdom, hear me, Celia.
Thy baths shall be the juice of July-flowers,
Spirit of roses, and of violets,
The milk of unicorns, and panthers' breath   215
Gathered in bags and mixed with Cretan wines.
Our drink shall be prepared gold and amber,
Which we will take until my roof whirl round
With the vertigo; and my dwarf shall dance,
My eunuch sing, my fool make up the antic.   220
Whilst we, in changèd shapes, act Ovid's tales,
Thou like Europa now, and I like Jove,
Then I like Mars, and thou like Erycine;
So of the rest, till we have quite run through,
And wearied all the fables of the gods.   225
Then will I have thee in more modern forms,
Attirèd like some sprightly dame of France,
Brave Tuscan lady, or proud Spanish beauty;
Sometimes unto the Persian Sophy's wife,

205 NATURE . . . KIND (*the phoenix*) *became extinct.*
213 JULY-FLOWERS *gillyflowers.*
215 PANTHERS' BREATH *N.*
220 ANTIC *grotesque dance.*
221 OVID'S TALES The Metamorphoses, *a series of stories dealing with human transformations.*
223 ERYCINE *Venus.*
229 SOPHY *ruler.*

230 Or the Grand Signior's mistress; and, for change,
To one of our most artful courtesans,
Or some quick Negro, or cold Russian;
And I will meet thee in as many shapes;
Where we may, so, transfuse our wand'ring souls [*Kissing her.*]

235 Out at our lips and score up sums of pleasures,
       That the curious shall not know
       How to tell them as they flow;
       And the envious, when they find
       What their number is, be pined.

240   *Celia.* If you have ears that will be pierced, or eyes
That can be opened, a heart may be touched,
Or any part that yet sounds man about you;
If you have touch of holy saints, or heaven,
Do me the grace to let me 'scape. If not,

245 Be bountiful and kill me. You do know
I am a creature hither ill betrayed
By one whose shame I would forget it were.
If you will deign me neither of these graces,
Yet feed your wrath, sir, rather than your lust,

250 It is a vice comes nearer manliness,
And punish that unhappy crime of nature,
Which you miscall my beauty: flay my face,
Or poison it with ointments for seducing
Your blood to this rebellion. Rub these hands

255 With what may cause an eating leprosy,

230 GRAND SIGNIOR *Sultan of Turkey, noted for cruelty.*
232 QUICK *lively.*
237 TELL *count.*
239 PINED *eaten up with envy.*
242 SOUNDS MAN *announces you to be a man (rather than beast).*
254 REBELLION *i.e. because reason and virtue should control passion, "blood."*
255 LEPROSY *any serious disease of the skin.*

128

E'en to my bones and marrow; anything
That may disfavour me, save in my honor,
And I will kneel to you, pray for you, pay down
A thousand hourly vows, sir, for your health;
Report, and think you virtuous—
    Volpone.   Think me cold,   260
Frozen, and impotent, and so report me?
That I had Nestor's hernia thou wouldst think.
I do degenerate and abuse my nation
To play with opportunity thus long;
I should have done the act, and then have parleyed.   265
Yield, or I'll force thee. [*He seizes her.*]
    Celia.   O! just God!
    Volpone.   In vain—
    Bonario. Forbear, foul ravisher! libidinous swine! *He leaps*
Free the forced lady, or thou diest, impostor.   *out from*
But that I am loth to snatch thy punishment   *where Mosca*
Out of the hand of justice, thou shouldst yet   *had placed* 270
Be made the timely sacrifice of vengeance,   *him.*
Before this altar, and this dross, thy idol.   [*Points to the gold.*]
Lady, let's quit the place, it is the den
Of villainy; fear nought, you have a guard;
And he ere long shall meet his just reward.   275
                    [*Exeunt Bonario & Celia.*]
    Volpone. Fall on me, roof, and bury me in ruin!
Become my grave, that wert my shelter! O!
I am unmasked, unspirited, undone,
Betrayed to beggary, to infamy—

257 DISFAVOUR *make the face ugly.*
262 NESTOR'S HERNIA *Nestor is the very old and wise Greek of the* Iliad—*the hernia suggests impotence.*
268 IMPOSTOR *pretender; but see N. to IV.6.24.*
275 HE *i.e. Volpone.*

Act III Scene viii

[*Enter Mosca, bleeding.*]

Mosca. Where shall I run, most wretched shame of men,
To beat out my unlucky brains?

    Volpone.   Here, here.

What! dost thou bleed?

    Mosca.   O, that his well-driven sword
Had been so courteous to have cleft me down
5 Unto the navel, ere I lived to see
My life, my hopes, my spirits, my patron, all
Thus desperately engagèd by my error.

    Volpone. Woe on thy fortune!

    Mosca.   And my follies, sir.

    Volpone. Th' hast made me miserable.

    Mosca.   And myself, sir.
10 Who would have thought he would have hearkened so?

    Volpone. What shall we do?

    Mosca.   I know not; if my heart
Could expiate the mischance, I'd pluck it out.
Will you be pleased to hang me, or cut my throat?
And I'll requite you, sir. Let's die like Romans,
15 Since we have lived like Grecians. *They knock without.*

    Volpone.   Hark! who's there?

---

7 ENGAGÈD *trapped.*

10 HE *i.e. Bonario.* HEARKENED *listened.*

14 REQUITE *do the same for.* ROMANS *referring to Roman custom of committing
suicide in adversity.*

15 GRECIANS *noted for dissolute living.*

I hear some footing; officers, the *Saffi*,
Come to apprehend us! I do feel the brand
Hissing already at my forehead; now,
Mine ears are boring.

    Mosca.   To your couch, sir; you
Make that place good, however. Guilty men [*Volpone lies down.*]   20
Suspect what they deserve still. [*Mosca opens door.*]
                      Signior Corbaccio!

16 FOOTING *footsteps.*
16 SAFFI *police.*
17–19 BRAND . . . BORING *branding on the forehead and cutting the ears was
    common punishment for criminals.*
20 MAKE . . . HOWEVER *maintain your disguise as a sick man whatever happens.*

Act III Scene ix

                [*Enter Corbaccio.*]
    Corbaccio. Why, how now, Mosca?
    Mosca.   O, undone, amazed, sir.
Your son, I know not by what accident,
Acquainted with your purpose to my patron,
Touching your will, and making him your heir,
Entered our house with violence, his sword drawn,   5
Sought for you, called you wretch, unnatural,
Vowed he would kill you.
    Corbaccio.   Me?
    Mosca.   Yes, and my patron.
    Corbaccio. This act shall disinherit him indeed.
Here is the will.
    Mosca.   'Tis well, sir.

1 AMAZED *confused.*
3 PURPOSE *intention.*

  Corbaccio.   Right and well.
10 Be you as careful now for me.
       [*Enter Voltore behind.*]
Mosca.   My life, sir,
Is not more tendered; I am only yours.
  Corbaccio. How does he? Will he die shortly, think'st thou?
  Mosca.   I fear
He'll outlast May.
  Corbaccio. Today?
  Mosca. [*Shouting.*] No, last out May, sir.
  Corbaccio. Couldst thou not gi' him a dram?
  Mosca.   O, by no means, sir.
15 *Corbaccio.* Nay, I'll not bid you.
  Voltore. [*Stepping forward.*] This is a knave, I see.
  Mosca. [*Aside.*] How! Signior Voltore! Did he hear me?
  Voltore.   Parasite!
  Mosca. Who's that? O, sir, most timely welcome.
  Voltore.   Scarce
To the discovery of your tricks, I fear.
You are his, only? And mine, also, are you not?
          [*Corbaccio wanders to the
          side of the stage and
20 *Mosca.* Who? I, sir?   stands there.*]
  Voltore.   You, sir. What device is this
About a will?
  Mosca. A plot for you, sir.
  Voltore.   Come,
Put not your foists upon me; I shall scent 'em.

---

10 CAREFUL *concerned for benefit.*
11 TENDERED *watched over.*
14 DRAM *drink (of poison).*
20 DEVICE *scheme.*
22 FOISTS *tricks, but word also means, "odor."*

Mosca. Did you not hear it?

Voltore.   Yes, I hear Corbaccio
Hath made your patron, there, his heir.

Mosca.   'Tis true,
By my device, drawn to it by my plot,   25
With hope—

Voltore.   Your patron should reciprocate?
And you have promised?

Mosca.   For your good I did, sir.
Nay, more, I told his son, brought, hid him here,
Where he might hear his father pass the deed;
Being persuaded to it by this thought, sir: 30
That the unnaturalness, first, of the act,
And then his father's oft disclaiming in him,
Which I did mean t' help on, would sure enrage him
To do some violence upon his parent.
On which the law should take sufficient hold,   35
And you be stated in a double hope.
Truth be my comfort, and my conscience,
My only aim was to dig you a fortune
Out of these two old, rotten sepulchres—

Voltore. I cry thee mercy, Mosca.

Mosca.   Worth your patience,   40
And your great merit, sir. And see the change!

Voltore. Why, what success?

Mosca.   Most hapless! you must help, sir.
Whilst we expected th' old raven, in comes

---

32 OFT . . . HIM *frequent denial of kinship.*

35 SUFFICIENT HOLD *i.e. punish him in such a way that he could not inherit.*

36 STATED *settled.* DOUBLE HOPE *i.e. inheriting Volpone's and Corbaccio's fortunes.*

40 CRY . . . MERCY *beg your pardon.*

42 SUCCESS *result.*

Corvino's wife, sent hither by her husband—

45 *Voltore.* What, with a present?

    Mosca.   No, sir, on visitation;

I'll tell you how anon—and staying long,

The youth he grows impatient, rushes forth,

Seizeth the lady, wounds me, makes her swear—

Or he would murder her, that was his vow—

50 T' affirm my patron to have done her rape,

Which how unlike it is, you see! and hence,

With that pretext he's gone t' accuse his father,

Defame my patron, defeat you—

    Voltore.   Where's her husband?

Let him be sent for straight.

    Mosca.   Sir, I'll go fetch him.

55 *Voltore.* Bring him to the *Scrutineo*.

    Mosca.   Sir, I will.

Voltore. This must be stopped.

    Mosca.   O, you do nobly, sir.

Alas, 'twas labored all, sir, for your good;

Nor was there want of counsel in the plot.

But Fortune can, at any time, o'erthrow

60 The projects of a hundred learned clerks, sir.

    Corbaccio. What's that?

                [Suddenly becoming aware that others are present.]

Voltore. [*To Corbaccio.*] Will 't please you, sir, to go along?

                      [Exeunt

                      Corbaccio and

                      Voltore.]

Mosca. [*To Volpone.*] Patron, go in and pray for our success.

Volpone. Need makes devotion; heaven your labor bless!

---

55 SCRUTINEO *law court in Senate House.*
60 CLERKS *learned men.*

Act IV Scene i

[*A street in Venice.*]
[*Enter Sir Politic and Peregrine.*]

Sir Politic. I told you, sir, it was a plot; you see
What observation is! You mentioned me
For some instructions: I will tell you, sir,
Since we are met here in this height of Venice,
Some few particulars I have set down   5
Only for this meridian, fit to be known
Of your crude traveler; and they are these.
I will not touch, sir, at your phrase, or clothes,
For they are old.
   Peregrine.   Sir, I have better.
   Sir Politic.   Pardon,
I meant as they are themes.
   Peregrine.   O, sir, proceed.   10
I'll slander you no more of wit, good sir.
   Sir Politic. First, for your garb, it must be grave and serious,

1 IT *Sir Pol apparently takes the entire mountebank scene as a plot.*
2 OBSERVATION *careful scrutiny of events.* MENTIONED *asked(?) N.*
4 HEIGHT *latitude.*
8 TOUCH . . . AT *deal with.* PHRASE *manner of speaking.*
10 THEMES *topics for discussion.*
12 GARB *bearing.*

Very reserved and locked; not tell a secret
On any terms, not to your father; scarce
15 A fable but with caution; make sure choice
Both of your company and discourse; beware
You never speak a truth—
    Peregrine.   How!
    Sir Politic.   Not to strangers,
For those be they you must converse with most;
Others I would not know, sir, but at distance,
20 So as I still might be a saver in 'em.
You shall have tricks, else, passed upon you hourly.
And then, for your religion, profess none,
But wonder at the diversity of all;
And, for your part, protest were there no other
25 But simply the laws o' th' land, you could content you.
Nick Machiavel and Monsieur Bodin both
Were of this mind. Then must you learn the use
And handling of your silver fork at meals,
The metal of your glass (these are main matters
30 With your Italian), and to know the hour
When you must eat your melons and your figs.
    Peregrine. Is that a point of state too?
    Sir Politic.   Here it is.
For your Venetian, if he see a man
Preposterous in the least, he has him straight;

13 NOT *do not.*
15 FABLE *story.*
19 KNOW *acknowledge.*
20 SO . . . 'EM "*So I might retain their friendship*'(?).
24–5 WERE . . . YOU *N.*
26 MACHIAVEL . . . BODIN *N.*
28 FORK *forks were fairly common in Italy, but not in England, at this time.*
29 METAL *material.* MAIN *primary.*
34 PREPOSTEROUS *incorrect.* STRAIGHT *at once.*

He has, he strips him. I'll acquaint you, sir.   35
I now have lived here 'tis some fourteen months;
Within the first week of my landing here,
All took me for a citizen of Venice,
I knew the forms so well—
   Peregrine.   [*Aside.*] And nothing else.
   Sir Politic. I had read Contarini, took me a house,   40
Dealt with my Jews to furnish it with movables—
Well, if I could but find one man, one man
To mine own heart, whom I durst trust, I would—
   Peregrine. What, what, sir?
   Sir Politic.   Make him rich, make him a fortune:
He should not think again. I would command it.   45
   Peregrine. As how?
   Sir Politic.   With certain projects that I have,
Which I may not discover.
   Peregrine.   [*Aside.*] If I had
But one to wager with, I would lay odds, now,
He tells me instantly.
   Sir Politic.   One is, and that
I care not greatly who knows, to serve the state   50
Of Venice with red herrings for three years,
And at a certain rate, from Rotterdam,
Where I have correspondence. There's a letter [*Showing a greasy*
Sent me from one o' th' States, and to that   *sheet of*
    purpose;   *paper.*]
He cannot write his name, but that's his mark.   55

40 CONTARINI *Cardinal Contarini (1483–1542) wrote a book on Venice which
    was translated into English in 1599.*
41 MOVABLES *furnishings.*
46 PROJECTS *N.*
47 DISCOVER *disclose.*
53 CORRESPONDENCE *commercial connections.*
54 STATES *Holland.* THAT PURPOSE *i.e. selling herring to Venice.*

Peregrine. He is a chandler?

Sir Politic.   No, a cheesemonger.

There are some other too with whom I treat

About the same negotiation;

And I will undertake it: for 'tis thus

60 I'll do 't with ease, I've cast it all. Your hoy

Carries but three men in her, and a boy;

And she shall make me three returns a year.

So, if there come but one of three, I save;

If two, I can defalk. But this is now

65 If my main project fail.

Peregrine.   Then you have others?

Sir Politic. I should be loath to draw the subtle air

Of such a place without my thousand aims.

I'll not dissemble, sir; where'er I come

I love to be considerative, and 'tis true

70 I have at my free hours thought upon

Some certain goods unto the state of Venice,

Which I do call my cautions; and, sir, which

I mean, in hope of pension, to propound

To the Great Council, then unto the Forty,

75 So to the Ten. My means are made already—

Peregrine. By whom?

Sir Politic.   Sir, one that though his place be **obscure**,

Yet he can sway, and they will hear him. He's

A *commendatore*.

56 CHANDLER *seller of candles. Peregrine is commenting on the greasiness of the paper.*

60 CAST *figured.* HOY *small Dutch coastal boat.*

64 DEFALK *retrench financially.*

69 CONSIDERATIVE *inquiring and thoughtful.*

72 CAUTIONS *precautions.*

73 PENSION *he hopes for a pension from the state as reward for his projects.*

74–5 GREAT . . . TEN *the ruling bodies of Venice in order of importance.*

Peregrine. What, a common sergeant?

Sir Politic. Sir, such as they are put it in their mouths
What they should say, sometimes, as well as greater.   80
I think I have my notes to show you— [*Searching his pockets.*]

Peregrine.   Good sir.

Sir Politic. But you shall swear unto me, on your gentry,
Not to anticipate—

Peregrine. I, sir?

Sir Politic.   Nor reveal
A circumstance—My paper is not with me.

Peregrine. O, but you can remember, sir.

Sir Politic.   My first is   85
Concerning tinderboxes. You must know
No family is here without its box.
Now, sir, it being so portable a thing,
Put case that you or I were ill affected
Unto the state; sir, with it in our pockets   90
Might not I go into the Arsenal?
Or you? Come out again? And none the wiser?

Peregrine. Except yourself, sir.

Sir Politic.   Go to, then. I therefore
Advertise to the state how fit it were
That none but such as were known patriots,   95
Sound lovers of their country, should be suffered
T' enjoy them in their houses; and even those
Sealed at some office, and at such a bigness
As might not lurk in pockets.

Peregrine.   Admirable!

79–80 "*Common sergeants as well as more important people sometimes tell the powerful what to think and say.*"

89 PUT CASE "*Say for example.*"

91 ARSENAL *famous Venetian building which housed all their ships and weapons.*

94 ADVERTISE *make known.*

97 THEM *i.e. tinderboxes.*

100   *Sir Politic.* My next is, how t' inquire, and be resolved
       By present demonstration, whether a ship
       Newly arrivèd from Syria, or from
       Any suspected part of all the Levant,
       Be guilty of the plague. And where they use
105   To lie out forty, fifty days, sometimes,
       About the *Lazaretto* for their trial,
       I'll save that charge and loss unto the merchant,
       And in an hour clear the doubt.
         Peregrine.   Indeed, sir!
         Sir Politic. Or——I will lose my labor.
         Peregrine.   My faith, that's much.
110   *Sir Politic.* Nay, sir, conceive me. 'Twill cost me, in onions,
       Some thirty livres—
         Peregrine.   Which is one pound sterling.
         Sir Politic. Beside my waterworks. For this I do, sir:
       First, I bring in your ship 'twixt two brick walls—
       But those the state shall venture. On the one
115 I strain me a fair tarpaulin, and in that
       I stick my onions, cut in halves; the other
       Is full of loopholes, out at which I thrust
       The noses of my bellows; and those bellows
       I keep, with waterworks, in perpetual motion,
120 Which is the easiest matter of a hundred.
       Now, sir, your onion, which doth naturally
       Attract th' infection, and your bellows blowing

---

101 PRESENT DEMONSTRATION *immediate experiment.*
104 GUILTY OF *infected with.* USE *are accustomed.*
106 LAZARETTO *a quarantine hospital.*
108 CLEAR THE DOUBT *make sure (whether they are infected).*
111 LIVRE *French coin.*
114 VENTURE *pay for.*
121–2 NATURALLY ATTRACT *onions were believed to collect plague infection.*

The air upon him, will show instantly
By his changed color if there be contagion,
Or else remain as fair as at the first.   125
Now 'tis known, 'tis nothing.
   Peregrine.   You are right, sir.
   Sir Politic. I would I had my note. [*Searching his pockets*]
   Peregrine   Faith, so would I.
But you ha' done well for once, sir.
   Sir Politic.   Were I false,
Or would be made so, I could show you reasons
How I could sell this state, now, to the Turk—   130
Spite of their galleys, or their—
               [*Still frantically searching his pocket.*]
   Peregrine.   Pray you, Sir Pol.
   Sir Politic. I have 'em not about me.
   Peregrine.   That I feared.
They're there, sir? [*Pulling a book from Sir Pol's pocket.*]
   Sir Politic.   No, this is my diary,
Wherein I note my actions of the day.
   Peregrine. Pray you let's see, sir. What is here?—"*Notandum*, 135
A rat had gnawn my spur leathers; notwithstanding,
I put on new and did go forth; but first
I threw three beans over the threshold. Item,
I went and bought two toothpicks, whereof one
I burst, immediately, in a discourse   140
With a Dutch merchant 'bout *ragion del stato*.
From him I went and paid a *moccenigo*

128 FALSE *traitorous.*
129 REASONS *feasible methods*(?).
131 THEIR *i.e. the Venetians'.*
133 DIARY *N.*
138 THREE BEANS *N.*
141 RAGION DEL STATO *political affairs.*
142 MOCCENIGO *coin of small value.*

141

For piecing my silk stockings; by the way
I cheapened sprats, and at St. Mark's I urined."
145 Faith, these are politic notes!
    Sir Politic.   Sir, I do slip
No action of my life, thus but I quote it.
    Peregrine. Believe me it is wise!
    Sir Politic.   Nay, sir, read forth.

143 PIECING *mending.*
144 CHEAPENED *bargained for.*
145 SLIP *allow to pass.*
146 THUS BUT *but in this manner.* QUOTE *note.*
147 FORTH *on.*

Act IV Scene ii

        [Enter Lady Wouldbe, Nano, and two Women.]
    Lady Wouldbe. Where should this loose knight be, trow? Sure,
    he's housed.
    Nano. Why, then he's fast.
    Lady Wouldbe.   Ay, he plays both with me.
I pray you stay. This heat will do more harm
To my complexion than his heart is worth.
5 I do not care to hinder, but to take him.
How it comes off! *[Rubbing her makeup.]*
    1st Woman.   My master's yonder. *[Pointing.]*
    Lady Wouldbe.   Where?
    2nd Woman. With a young gentleman.
    Lady Wouldbe.   That same's the party!
In man's apparel! Pray you, sir, jog my knight.

1 LOOSE *lascivious.* HOUSED *i.e. in a bawdy house.*
2 FAST *caught.* BOTH *fast and loose, see N. to I.2.8.*
8 JOG *poke(?), remind.*

142

I will be tender to his reputation,
However he demerit.
    Sir Politic.   My lady!
    Peregrine.   Where?   10
    Sir Politic. 'Tis she indeed; sir, you shall know her. She is,
Were she not mine, a lady of that merit
For fashion, and behavior, and for beauty
I durst compare—
    Peregrine.   It seems you are not jealous,
That dare commend her.
    Sir Politic.   Nay, and for discourse—   15
    Peregrine. Being your wife, she cannot miss that.
    Sir Politic. [*The parties join.*]   Madam,
Here is a gentleman; pray you, use him fairly;
He seems a youth, but he is—
    Lady Wouldbe.   None?
    Sir Politic.   Yes, one
Has put his face as soon into the world—
    Lady Wouldbe. You mean, as early? But today?
    Sir Politic.   How's this?   20
    Lady Wouldbe. Why, in this habit, sir; you apprehend me!
Well, Master Wouldbe, this doth not become you.
I had thought the odor, sir, of your good name
Had been more precious to you; that you would not
Have done this dire massàcre on your honor,   25
One of your gravity, and rank besides!
But knights, I see, care little for the oath
They make to ladies, chiefly their own ladies.

---

10 DEMERIT *does not deserve (care for his reputation).*
15 DISCOURSE *conversation.*
16 MISS *lack.*
21 HABIT *dress.*
25 MASSÀCRE *accented on second syllable.*

    Sir Politic. Now, by my spurs, the symbol of my knighthood—

30   *Peregrine.* [*Aside.*] Lord, how his brain is humbled for an oath!

    Sir Politic. I reach you not.

    Lady Wouldbe.   Right sir, your policy

May bear it through thus. [*To Peregrine.*] Sir, a word with you,

I would be loath to contest publicly

With any gentlewoman, or to seem

35 Froward, or violent, as *The Courtier* says.

It comes too near rusticity in a lady,

Which I would shun by all means. And, however

I may deserve from Master Wouldbe, yet

T' have one fair gentlewoman, thus, be made

40 Th' unkind instrument to wrong another,

And one she knows not, ay, and to persèver,

In my poor judgment, is not warranted

From being a solecism in our sex,

If not in manners.

    Peregrine.   How is this!

    Sir Politic.   Sweet madam,

45 Come nearer to your aim.

    Lady Wouldbe.   Marry, and will, sir.

Since you provoke me with your impudence

And laughter of your light land-siren here,

30 HUMBLED *N.*

31 REACH *understand.* POLICY *craft.*

32 BEAR IT THROUGH *carry it off.*

35 FROWARD *perverse.* THE COURTIER *N.*

36 RUSTICITY *country manners, vulgarity.*

41 PERSÈVER *accented on second syllable.*

42 WARRANTED *guaranteed (against).*

43 SOLECISM . . . SEX *sexual impropriety—the lady's language is overcharged.*

45 COME . . . AIM *make your point more clearly.*

47 LIGHT *immoral.*

(handwritten margin notes: "...then were... contrasted + modeled" / "(the confusion of the sexes furthers theme of unnaturalness)")

Your Sporus, your hermaphrodite—

   Peregrine.   What's here?

Poetic fury and historic storms!

   Sir Politic. The gentleman, believe it, is of worth,   50

And of our nation.

   Lady Wouldbe.   Ay, your Whitefriars nation!

Come, I blush for you, Master Wouldbe, ay;

And am ashamed you should ha' no more forehead

Than thus to be the patron, or St. George,

To a lewd harlot, a base fricatrice,   55

A female devil in a male outside.

   Sir Politic.   Nay,

And you be such a one, I must bid adieu

To your delights. The case appears too liquid.   [*Exit.*]

   Lady Wouldbe. Ay, you may carry't clear, with your state-face!

But for your carnival concupiscence,   60

Who here is fled for liberty of conscience,

From furious persecution of the marshal,

Her will I disc'ple.

   Peregrine.   This is fine, i' faith!

And do you use this often? Is this part

(handwritten margin note near line 51: "a liberty or area exempt from the law in London")

48 SPORUS *N.*

51 WHITEFRIARS NATION *N.*

53 FOREHEAD *shame.*

55 FRICATRICE *literally a massage, but also slang for whore.*

56-8 NAY . . . LIQUID *N.*

59 CARRY'T CLEAR *carry on your pretense (of innocence).* STATE-FACE *grave, official manner—Lady Wouldbe seems to take her husband's pretenses to statesmanship seriously.*

60 CARNIVAL CONCUPISCENCE *licentious wench—Lady Wouldbe is close to using malapropisms.*

61 LIBERTY OF CONSCIENCE *i.e. freedom to practice her bawdy trade.*

62 MARSHAL *court officer and keeper of prisons.*

63 DISC'PLE *discipline.*

64 USE THIS *act in this way.*

65 Of your wit's exercise, 'gainst you have occasion?
  Madam—
      Lady Wouldbe Go to sir.
      Peregrine.   Do you hear me, lady?
  Why, if your knight have set you to beg shirts,
  Or to invite me home, you might have done it
  A nearer way by far.
      Lady Wouldbe.   This cannot work you
70 Out of my snare.
      Peregrine.   Why, am I in it, then?
  Indeed, your husband told me you were fair,
  And so you are; only your nose inclines—
  That side that's next the sun—to the queen-apple.
      Lady Wouldbe. This cannot be endured by any patience.

65 'GAINST *in preparation for a time when.* OCCASION *real need.*
69 NEARER *more direct.*
71 FAIR *light complexioned—considered an attribute of beauty.*
72 INCLINES *tends.*
73 QUEEN-APPLE *i.e. bright red.*

Act IV Scene iii

[*Enter Mosca.*]
  Mosca. What's the matter, madam?
  Lady Wouldbe.   If the Senate
  Right not my quest in this, I will protest 'em
  To all the world no aristocracy.
      Mosca. What is the injury, lady?
      Lady Wouldbe.   Why, the callet
5 You told me of, here I have ta'en disguised.

2 QUEST *petition.* PROTEST *publish.*
4 CALLET *prostitute.*

146

Mosca. Who? This! What means your ladyship? The creature
I mentioned to you is apprehended, now
Before the Senate. You shall see her—

   Lady Wouldbe.   Where?

   Mosca. I'll bring you to her. This young gentleman,
I saw him land this morning at the port.   10

   Lady Wouldbe. Is't possible? How has my judgment wandered!
Sir, I must, blushing, say to you, I have erred;
And plead your pardon.

   Peregrine.   What, more changes yet?

   Lady Wouldbe. I hope y' ha' not the malice to remember
A gentlewoman's passion. If you stay   15
In Venice, here, please you to use me, sir—

   Mosca. Will you go, madam?

   Lady Wouldbe.   Pray you, sir, use me. In faith,
The more you see me, the more I shall conceive
You have forgot our quarrel.

            [*Exeunt Lady Wouldbe, Mosca, Nano and Women.*]

   Peregrine.   This is rare!
Sir Politic Wouldbe? No, Sir Politic Bawd,   20
To bring me, thus, acquainted with his wife!
Well, wise Sir Pol, since you have practiced thus
Upon my freshmanship, I'll try your salt-head,
What proof it is against a counterplot.   [*Exit.*]

16 USE *N.*
20 BAWD *pander.*
21 BRING *make.*
22 PRACTICED *intrigued.*
23 FRESHMANSHIP *newness, greenness—Peregrine seems to believe that Sir Pol
has been having a joke at his expense.* SALT-HEAD *experienced in the world—
spoken ironically.*

Act IV Scene iv

[*The Scrutineo, the Venetian court of law.*]
[*Enter Voltore, Corbaccio, Corvino, and Mosca.*]

Voltore. Well, now you know the carriage of the business,
Your constancy is all that is required,
Unto the safety of it.

Mosca.　　　　　　Is the lie
Safely conveyed amongst us? Is that sure?
5 Knows every man his burden?

Corvino.　　　　　　Yes.

Mosca.　　　　　　Then shrink not.

Corvino. [*Aside to Mosca.*] But knows the advocate the truth?

Mosca.　　　　　　　　　　O sir,
By no means. I devised a formal tale
That salved your reputation. But be valiant, sir.

Corvino. I fear no one but him, that this his pleading
10 Should make him stand for a co-heir—

Mosca.　　　　　　Co-halter!
Hang him, we will but use his tongue, his noise,
As we do Croaker's here. [*Pointing to Corbaccio.*]

Corvino.　　　Ay, what shall he do?

Mosca. When we ha' done, you mean?

Corvino.　　　　　　Yes.

---

1 CARRIAGE *management, way of handling.*
4 CONVEYED *spread to all.*
5 BURDEN *refrain in a song, i.e. what he is to say at the right moment.*
7 FORMAL *"elaborately constructed, circumstantial"* (OED).
8 SALVED *saved.*

(part of the end of [illegible] cannot [illegible] in the play) ✓

Mosca.   Why, we'll think:
Sell him for mummia, he's half dust already.   [*Turns away from*
Do not you smile to see this buffalo,   *Corvino and*   15
How he doth sport it with his head?—I should, *speaks to Voltore.*]
If all were well and past. (*To Corbaccio.*) Sir, only you
Are he that shall enjoy the crop of all,
And these not know for whom they toil.

  Corbaccio.   Ay, peace.

  Mosca. (*To Corvino.*) But you shall eat it.—Much!—

(ironical view)   (*To Voltore.*) Worshipful sir,   20
Mercury sit upon your thund'ring tongue,
Or the French Hercules, and make your language
As conquering as his club, to beat along,
As with a tempest, flat, our adversaries;
But much more yours, sir.

  Voltore.   Here they come, ha' done.   25

  Mosca. I have another witness if you need, sir,
I can produce.

  Voltore.   Who is it?

  Mosca.   Sir, I have her.

---

14 MUMMIA *N.*
15 BUFFALO *referring to Corvino's horns.*
16 SPORT . . . HEAD *play about unconscious of his horns.*
20 EAT IT *i.e. enjoy all the gold.* MUCH! *not at all.*
21 MERCURY *god of eloquence, but also of thieves.*
22 FRENCH HERCULES *another symbol of eloquence.*
27 HER *i.e. Lady Wouldbe.*

Act IV Scene v

[*Enter four Avocatori, Bonario, Celia, Notario, Commendatori,*
and Others.]

    1st Avocatore. The like of this the Sentate never heard of.

    2nd Avocatore. 'Twill come most strange to them when we
report it.

    4th Avocatore. The gentlewoman has been ever held
Of unreprovèd name.

    3rd Avocatore.   So the young man.

5   *4th Avocatore.* The more unnatural part, that of his father.

    2nd Avocatore. More of the husband.

    1st Avocatore.   I not know to give
His act a name, it is so monstrous!

    4th Avocatore. But the impostor, he is a thing created
T' exceed example.

    1st Avocatore.   And all after-times!

10   *2nd Avocatore.* I never heard a true voluptuary
Described but him.

    3rd Avocatore.   Appear yet those were cited?

    Notario. All but the old magnifico, Volpone.

    1st Avocatore. Why is not he here?

    Mosca.   Please your fatherhoods,
Here is his advocate. Himself's so weak,

15 So feeble—

    4th Avocatore. What are you?

5 PART *i.e. to disinherit his son.*

7 MONSTROUS *trisyllabic: mon-ster-ous.*

9 EXAMPLE *the outstanding instances provided by art and history.* AFTER-
TIMES *the future.*

11 CITED *summoned.*

12 MAGNIFICO *nobleman.*

Bonario.   His parasite,   15
His knave, his pander! I beseech the court
He may be forced to come, that your grave eyes
May bear strong witness of his strange impostures.
    Voltore. Upon my faith and credit with your virtues,
He is not able to endure the air.   20
    2nd Avocatore. Bring him, however.
    3rd Avocatore.   We will see him.
    4th Avocatore.   Fetch him.
    Voltore. Your fatherhoods' fit pleasures be obeyed,
But sure the sight will rather move your pities
Than indignation. May it please the court,
In the meantime he may be heard in me!   25
I know this place most void of prejudice,
And therefore crave it, since we have no reason
To fear our truth should hurt our cause.
    3rd Avocatore.   Speak free.
    Voltore. Then know, most honored fathers, I must now
Discover to your strangely abusèd ears   30
The most prodigious and most frontless piece
Of solid impudence, and treachery,
That ever vicious nature yet brought forth
To shame the state of Venice. This lewd woman,
                              [*Pointing to Celia.*]
That wants no artificial looks or tears   35
To help the visor she has now put on,
Hath long been known a close adulteress

22 FATHERHOODS' *N.*
27 IT *i.e. to be heard.*
31 FRONTLESS *shameless.*
35 WANTS *lacks.*
36 VISOR *mask. Celia is crying and distraught, and Voltore is accusing her of pretending.*
37 CLOSE *secret.*

Act IV Scene v

To that lascivious youth, there; [*Pointing to Bonario.*]

not suspected,

I say, but known, and taken, in the act,

40 With him; and by this man, the easy husband,

[*Pointing to Corvino.*]

Pardoned; whose timeless bounty makes him now

Stand here, the most unhappy, innocent person

That ever man's own goodness made accused.

For these, not knowing how to owe a gift

45 Of that dear grace but with their shame, being placed

So above all powers of their gratitude,

Began to hate the benefit, and in place

Of thanks, devise t' extirp the memory

Of such an act. Wherein, I pray your fatherhoods

50 To observe the malice, yea, the rage of creatures

Discovered in their evils; and what heart

Such take, even from their crimes. But that anon

Will more appear. This gentleman, the father,

[*Pointing to Corbaccio.*]

Hearing of this foul fact, with many others,

55 Which daily struck at his too tender ears,

And grieved in nothing more than that he could not

Preserve himself a parent (his son's ills

Growing to that strange flood) at last decreed

To disinherit him.

45 DEAR GRACE *rich value.*

45-6 BEING . . . GRATITUDE "*forgiveness is so rare a virtue that these base creatures cannot comprehend it and be grateful.*"

47 BENEFIT *i.e. Corvino's forgiveness.*

48 EXTIRP *eradicate.*

54 FACT *crime—Latin facinus.*

56 GRIEVED . . . MORE "*nothing grieved him more.*"

57 ILLS *wrongdoings.*

58 GROWING . . . FLOOD *increasing to such great unnaturalness.*

152

1st Avocatore.   These be strange turns!

2nd Avocatore. The young man's fame was ever fair and honest.   60

Voltore. So much more full of danger is his vice,
That can beguile so under shade of virtue.
But as I said, my honored sires, his father
Having this settled purpose—by what means
To him betrayed, we know not—and this day   65
Appointed for the deed, that parricide,
I cannot style him better, by confederacy
Preparing this his paramour to be there,
Entered Volpone's house—who was the man,
Your fatherhoods must understand, designed   70
For the inheritance—there sought his father.
But with what purpose sought he him, my lords?
I tremble to pronounce it, that a son
Unto a father, and to such a father,
Should have so foul, felonious intent: 75
It was, to murder him! When, being prevented
By his more happy absence, what then did he?
Not check his wicked thoughts? No, now new deeds—
Mischief doth ever end where it begins—
An act of horror, fathers! He dragged forth   80
The agèd gentleman, that had there lain bed-rid
Three years, and more, out off his innocent couch,
Naked, upon the floor, there left him; wounded
His servant in the face; and, with this strumpet,
The stale to his forged practice, who was glad   85

59 TURNS *events.*
60 FAME *reputation.*
62 SHADE *cover, pretense.*
65 HIM *i.e. Bonario.*
67 CONFEDERACY *secret agreement.*
70 DESIGNED *designated.*
85 STALE *lure.* FORGED PRACTICE *contrived scheme.*

To be so active—I shall here desire
Your fatherhoods to note but my collections
As most remarkable—thought at once to stop
His father's ends, discredit his free choice
90 In the old gentleman, redeem themselves
By laying infamy upon this man,
To whom, with blushing, they should owe their lives.

    1st Avocatore. What proofs have you of this?

    Bonario.   Most honored fathers,
I humbly crave there be no credit given
95 To this man's mercenary tongue.

    2nd Avocatore.   Forbear.

    Bonario. His soul moves in his fee.

    3rd Avocatore.   O, sir!

    Bonario.   This fellow,
For six sols more would plead against his Maker.

    1st Avocatore. You do forget yourself.

    Voltore.   Nay, nay, grave fathers,
Let him have scope. Can any man imagine
100 That he will spare's accuser, that would not
Have spared his parent?

    1st Avocatore.   Well, produce your proofs.

    Celia. I would I could forget I were a creature!

    Voltore. Signor Corbaccio!

    4th Avocatore.   What is he?

    Voltore.   The father.

    2nd Avocatore. Has he had an oath?

87 COLLECTIONS *conclusions.*
89 ENDS *intentions.*
90 IN *of.* OLD GENTLEMAN *i.e. Volpone.*
91 THIS MAN *i.e. Corvino.*
92 OWE *acknowledge due.*
97 SOLS *coins of small value.*
99 SCOPE *freedom (to insult).*

Act IV Scene v

Notario.   Yes.

Corbaccio.   What must I do now?

Notario. Your testimony's craved.

Corbaccio. [*Cupping his ear.*]   Speak to the knave?   105
I'll ha' my mouth first stopped with earth. My heart
Abhors his knowledge. I disclaim in him.

    1st Avocatore. But for what cause?

    Corbaccio.   The mere portent of nature.
He is an utter stranger to my loins.

    Bonario. Have they made you to this?

    Corbaccio.   I will not hear thee,   110
Monster of men, swine, goat, wolf, parricide!
Speak not, thou viper.

    Bonario.   Sir, I will sit down,
And rather wish my innocence should suffer,
Than I resist the authority of a father.

    Voltore. Signor Corvino!

    2nd Avocatore.   This is strange.

    1st Avocatore.   Who's this?   115

    Notario. The husband.

    4th Avocatore.   Is he sworn?

    Notario.   He is.

    3rd Avocatore.   Speak, then.

    Corvino. This woman, please your fatherhoods, is a whore
Of most hot exercise, more than a partridge,
Upon recòrd—

    1st Avocatore. No more.

    Corvino.   Neighs like a jennet.

107 HIS KNOWLEDGE *knowing him.* DISCLAIM IN HIM *deny kinship to him.*
108 MERE PORTENT *complete monster.*
110 MADE . . . THIS *wrought you to this shape (i.e. a parent denying his son).*
118 HOT EXERCISE *frequent and passionate activity.* PARTRIDGE *believed to be an extremely lecherous bird.*
119 UPON RECÒRD *generally known and acknowledged.*

155

120   *Notario.* Preserve the honor of the court.

      Corvino.   I shall,

And modesty of your most reverend ears.

And, yet, I hope that I may say these eyes

Have seen her glued unto that piece of cedar,

That fine, well-timbered gallant; and that here   [*Tapping his*

125 The letters may be read, thorough the horn,   *forehead.*]

That make the story perfect.

      Mosca.   Excellent, sir.

                          [*Mosca and Corvino whisper.*]

      Corvino. There is no shame in this now, is there?

      Mosca.   None.

      Corvino. Or if I said I hoped that she were onward

To her damnation, if there be a hell

130 Greater than whore and woman; a good Catholic

May make the doubt.

      3rd Avocatore.   His grief hath made him frantic.

      1st Avocatore. Remove him hence. *She* [*Celia*] *swoons.*

      2nd Avocatore.   Look to the woman.

      Corvino.   Rare!

Prettily feigned! Again!

      4th Avocatore.   Stand from about her.

      1st Avocatore. Give her the air.

      3rd Avocatore. [*To Mosca.*]   What can you say?

      Mosca.   My wound,

135 May 't please your wisdoms, speaks for me, received

In aid of my good patron, when he missed

124 WELL-TIMBERED GALLANT *handsome young man* (*i.e. Bonario*).

125 LETTERS . . . HORN *N.* THOROUGH *through.*

126 PERFECT *complete.*

128 ONWARD *well along.*

131 MAKE THE DOUBT *question* (*whether whore, woman, and hell be not equi-valent*).

136 HE *i.e. Bonario.*

His sought-for father, when that well-taught dame
Had her cue given her to cry out a rape.
  Bonario. O most laid impudence! Fathers—
  3rd Avocatore.   Sir, be silent,
You had your hearing free, so must they theirs.   140
  2nd Avocatore. I do begin to doubt th' imposture here.
  4th Avocatore. This woman has too many moods.
  Voltore.   Grave fathers,
She is a creature of a most professed
And prostituted lewdness.
  Corvino.   Most impetuous,
Unsatisfied, grave fathers!
  Voltore.   May her feignings   145
Not take your wisdoms; but this day she baited
A stranger, a grave knight, with her loose eyes
And more lascivious kisses. This man saw 'em
Together on the water in a gondola.
  Mosca. Here is the lady herself that saw 'em too,   150
Without; who, then, had in the open streets
Pursued them, but for saving her knight's honor.
  1st Avocatore. Produce that lady. [*Mosca beckons to the wings.*]
  2nd Avocatore.   Let her come.
  4th Avocatore.   These things.
They strike with wonder!
  3rd Avocatore.   I am turned a stone!

139 LAID *carefully planned.*
140 FREE *without interference.*
143 PROFESSED *open.*
146 BUT *only.* BAITED *enticed.*
147 LOOSE *lewd.*
151 WITHOUT *outside.*

Act IV Scene vi

[*Enter Lady Wouldbe.*]

Mosca. Be resolute, madam.

Lady Wouldbe. [*Pointing to Celia.*] Ay, this same is she.
Out, thou chameleon harlot! Now thine eyes
Vie tears with the hyena. Dar'st thou look
Upon my wrongèd face? I cry your pardons. [*To the Court.*]
5 I fear I have forgettingly transgressed
Against the dignity of the court—

    2nd Avocatore.   No, madam.

Lady Wouldbe. And been exorbitant—

    4th Avocatore.   You have not, lady.
These proofs are strong.

    Lady Wouldbe.   Surely, I had no purpose
To scandalize your honors, or my sex's.

10 *3rd Avocatore.* We do believe it.

    Lady Wouldbe.   Surely, you may believe it.

    2nd Avocatore. Madam, we do.

    Lady Wouldbe.   Indeed, you may; my breeding
Is not so coarse—

    4th Avocatore.   We know it.

    Lady Wouldbe.   To offend
With pertinacy—

    3rd Avocatore.   Lady—

    Lady Wouldbe.   Such a presence.
No, surely,

2–3 CHAMELEON, HYENA *N.*

7 EXORBITANT *disorderly.*

8 THESE PROOFS *i.e. those offered for Celia and Bonario's guilt.*

13 PERTINACY *pertinacity.*

1st Avocatore. We well think it.

Lady Wouldbe.　　　　　You may think it.

1st Avocatore. Let her o'ercome. [*To Bonario.*] What witnesses
have you　　　　　　　　　　　　　　　　　　　15
To make good your report?

Bonario.　　　　　　Our consciences.

Celia. And heaven, that never fails the innocent.

4th Avocatore. These are no testimonies.

Bonario.　　　　　　　　　　　Not in your courts,
Where multitude and clamor overcomes.

1st Avocatore. Nay, then you do wax insolent.

　　　　　　Volpone is brought in, as impotent.

Voltore.　　　　　　　　　　　Here, here,　20
The testimony comes that will convince,
And put to utter dumbness their bold tongues.
See here, grave fathers, here's the ravisher,
The rider on men's wives, the great impostor,
The grand voluptuary! Do you not think　　　　25
These limbs should affect venery? Or these eyes
Covet a concubine? Pray you, mark these hands.
Are they not fit to stroke a lady's breasts?
Perhaps he doth dissemble!

Bonario.　　　　　So he does.

Voltore. Would you ha' him tortured?

Bonario.　　　　　　　I would have him proved.　30

Voltore. Best try him, then, with goads, or burning irons;

15 O'ERCOME *conquer (in exchange of formalities).*

16 MAKE GOOD *verify.*

19 MULTITUDE *the larger number (swearing the same story).* CLAMOR *loudness.*

SD IMPOTENT *completely disabled—he is presumably lying in a litter.*

24 GREAT IMPOSTOR *N.*

26 AFFECT VENERY *care for lust.*

30 PROVED *tested.*

Put him to the strappado. I have heard
The rack hath cured the gout. Faith, give it him
And help him of a malady; be courteous.
35 I'll undertake, before these honored fathers,
He shall have yet as many left diseases
As she has known adulterers, or thou strumpets.
O my most equal hearers, if these deeds,
Acts of this bold and most exorbitant strain,
40 May pass with sufferance, what one citizen
But owes the forfeit of his life, yea, fame,
To him that dares traduce him? Which of you
Are safe, my honored fathers? I would ask,
With leave of your grave fatherhoods, if their plot
45 Have any face or color like to truth?
Or if, unto the dullest nostril here,
It smell not rank and most abhorrèd slander?
I crave your care of this good gentleman,
Whose life is much endangered by their fable;
50 And as for them, I will conclude with this:
That vicious persons when they are hot and fleshed
In impious acts, their constancy abounds:
Damnèd deeds are done with greatest confidence.
　　　1st *Avocatore*. Take 'em to custody, and sever them.

　　　　　　　　　　　[*Celia and Bonario are taken out.*]

---

32 STRAPPADO *a form of torture in which the victim is hoisted up by his arms, which are first tied behind him, and then dropped.*
34 OF *be rid of.*
39 EXORBITANT STRAIN *disordered type.*
40 PASS . . . SUFFERANCE *be permitted and condoned.*
45 FACE OR COLOR *appearance or seeming.*
49 FABLE *falsehood.*
51 FLESHED *hardened, confirmed.*
52 CONSTANCY *firm determination.*

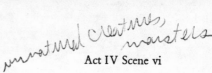

Act IV Scene vi

2nd Avocatore. 'Tis pity two such prodigies should live.   55
1st Avocatore. Let the old gentleman be returned with care.
I'm sorry our credulity wronged him.
                                [Exeunt Officers with Volpone.]
4th Avocatore. These are two creatures!
3rd Avocatore.   I have an earthquake in me!
2nd Avocatore. Their shame, even in their cradles, fled their faces.
4th Avocatore. [*To Voltore.*] You've done a worthy service to
    the state, sir,   60
In their discovery.
1st Avocatore.   You shall hear ere night
What punishment the court decrees upon 'em.
Voltore. We thank your fatherhoods.—
                                [Exeunt Court Officials.]
                          How like you it?
Mosca.   Rare.
I'd ha' your tongue, sir, tipped with gold for this;
I'd ha' you be the heir to the whole city;   65
The earth I'd have want men, ere you want living.
They're bound to erect your statue in St. Mark's.
                          [Voltore moves to one side.]
Signor Corvino, I would have you go
And show yourself, that you have conquered.
Corvino.   Yes.
Mosca. It was much better that you should profess   70
Yourself a cuckold, thus, than that the other
Should have been proved.
Corvino.   Nay, I considered that.
Now, it is her fault.
Mosca.   Then, it had been yours.

55 PRODIGIES *unnatural creatures, monsters.*
66 LIVING *income.*
71 OTHER *i.e. that he was pander for his wife.*

161

Corvino. True. I do doubt this advocate still.

Mosca.   I' faith,

75 You need not; I dare ease you of that care.

Corvino. I trust thee, Mosca.

Mosca.   As your own soul, sir.

                                  [*Exit Corvino.*]

Corbaccio.   Mosca!

Mosca. Now for your business, sir.

Corbaccio.   How! Ha' you business?

Mosca. Yes, yours, sir.

Corbaccio.   O, none else?

Mosca.   None else, not I.

Corbaccio. Be careful then.

Mosca.   Rest you with both your eyes, sir.

80   *Corbaccio.* Dispatch it.

Mosca.   Instantly.

Corbaccio.   And look that all

Whatever be put in: jewels, plate, moneys,

Household stuff, bedding, curtains.

Mosca.   Curtain-rings, sir;

Only the advocate's fee must be deducted.

Corbaccio. I'll pay him now; you'll be too prodigal.

85   *Mosca.* Sir, I must tender it.

Corbaccio.   Two chequins is well?

Mosca. No, six, sir.

Corbaccio.   'Tis too much.

Mosca.   He talked a great while,

You must consider that, sir.

74 DOUBT *suspect.*

78 NONE *no one.*

79 REST . . . EYES *"Don't worry about a thing."*

80 DISPATCH *be quick about.*

81 IN *i.e. in the inventory of Volpone's goods.*

85 TENDER *give.*

Corbaccio.   Well, there's three—
Mosca. I'll give it him.
Corbaccio.   Do so, and there's for thee.
                    [*Gives Mosca money and exits.*]
     Mosca. Bountiful bones! What horrid, strange offense
Did he commit 'gainst nature in his youth,   90
Worthy this age? [*To Voltore.*] You see, sir, how I work
Unto your ends; take you no notice.
     Voltore.   No,
I'll leave you.
     Mosca.   All is yours, [*Exit Voltore.*] —the devil and all,
Good advocate!— [*To Lady Wouldbe.*] Madam, I'll bring you
     home.
     Lady Wouldbe. No, I'll go see your patron.
     Mosca.   That you shall not. 95
I'll tell you why: my purpose is to urge
My patron to reform his will, and for
The zeal you've shown today, whereas before
You were but third or fourth, you shall be now
Put in the first; which would appear as begged   100
If you were present. Therefore—
     Lady Wouldbe.   You shall sway me.
                              [*Exeunt.*]

89 BOUNTIFUL BONES *this may be an exclamation of surprise at the physical
     and moral ugliness of Corbaccio, or it may refer ironically to his stinginess.*
91 WORTHY THIS AGE *"to have justified his horrible state in old age."*
97 REFORM *rewrite.*
101 SWAY *persuade.*

163

Act V Scene i

[*Volpone's house. Enter Volpone.*]

Volpone. Well, I am here, and all this brunt is past.
I ne'er was in dislike with my disguise
Till this fled moment. Here, 'twas good, in private,
But in your public—*Cavè*, whilst I breathe.
5 'Fore God, my left leg 'gan to have the cramp,
And I apprehended, straight, some power had struck me
With a dead palsy. Well, I must be merry
And shake it off. A many of these fears
Would put me into some villainous disease
10 Should they come thick upon me. I'll prevent 'em.
Give me a bowl of lusty wine to fright
This humor from my heart. Hum, hum, hum! *He drinks.*
'Tis almost gone already; I shall conquer.
Any device, now, of rare, ingenious knavery
15 That would possess me with a violent laughter,
Would make me up again. So, so, so, so. *Drinks again.*
This heat is life; 'tis blood by this time! Mosca!

1 BRUNT *confusion, crisis.*
3 FLED *past.*
4 CAVÈ *beware.*
6 APPREHENDED *felt.* STRAIGHT *at once.*
16 MAKE ME UP *restore me.*
17 HEAT . . . TIME *N.*

Act V Scene ii

[*Enter Mosca.*]

Mosca. How now, sir? Does the day look clear again?
Are we recovered? and wrought out of error
Into our way, to see our path before us?
Is our trade free once more?
Volpone.   Exquisite Mosca!
Mosca. Was it not carried learnedly?
Volpone.   And stoutly.   5
Good wits are greatest in extremities.
    Mosca. It were a folly beyond thought to trust
Any grand act unto a cowardly spirit.
You are not taken with it enough, methinks?
    Volpone. O, more than if I had enjoyed the wench.   10
The pleasure of all womankind's not like it.
    Mosca. Why, now you speak, sir! We must here be fixed;
Here we must rest. This is our masterpiece;
We cannot think to go beyond this.
    Volpone.   True,
Th'ast played thy prize, my precious Mosca.
    Mosca.   Nay, sir,   15
To gull the court—
    Volpone.   And quite divert the torrent
Upon the innocent.
    Mosca.   Yes, and to make
So rare a music out of discords—

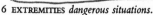

6 EXTREMITIES *dangerous situations.*
7 BEYOND THOUGHT *unthinkable.*
16 GULL *trick.* TORRENT *i.e. the law.*
18 DISCORDS *referring to the various fools each striving to be sole heir.*

Volpone.   Right.

That yet to me 's the strangest; how th'ast borne it!

20 That these, being so divided 'mongst themselves,

Should not scent somewhat, or in me or thee,

Or doubt their own side.

    Mosca.   True, they will not see't.

Too much light blinds 'em, I think. Each of 'em

Is so possessed and stuffed with his own hopes

25 That anything unto the contrary,

Never so true, or never so apparent,

Never so palpable, they will resist it—

    Volpone. Like a temptation of the devil.

    Mosca.   Right, sir.

Merchants may talk of trade, and your great signiors

30 Of land that yields well; but if Italy

Have any glebe more fruitful than these fellows,

I am deceived. Did not your advocate rare?

    Volpone. O—"My most honored fathers, my grave fathers,

Under correction of your fatherhoods,

35 What face of truth is here? If these strange deeds

May pass, most honored fathers"—I had much ado

To forbear laughing.

    Mosca.   'T seemed to me you sweat, sir.

    Volpone. In troth, I did a little.

    Mosca.   But confess, sir;

Were you not daunted?

    Volpone.   In good faith, I was

---

19 BORNE *managed.*

21 OR . . . OR *either . . . or.*

23 LIGHT *i.e. their greed and hopes.*

31 GLEBE *land.*

32 RARE *rarely.*

33–6 *See note to* IV.5.22.

A little in a mist, but not dejected;   40
Never but still myself.
   Mosca.   I think it, sir.
Now, so truth help me, I must needs say this, sir,
And out of conscience for your advocate:
He's taken pains, in faith, sir, and deserved,
In my poor judgment, I speak it under favor,   45
Not to contrary you, sir, very richly—
Well—to be cozened.
   Volpone.   Troth, and I think so too,
By that I heard him in the latter end.
   Mosca. O, but before, sir, had you heard him first
Draw it to certain heads, then aggravate,   50
Then use his vehement figures—I looked still
When he would shift a shirt; and doing this
Out of pure love, no hope of gain—
   Volpone.   'Tis right.
I cannot answer him, Mosca, as I would,
Not yet; but for thy sake, at thy entreaty,   55
I will begin e'en now to vex 'em all,
This very instant.

40 MIST *dimness of eyesight caused by bodily disorders.*
41 THINK *believe.*
45 UNDER FAVOR *with permission.*
47 COZENED *bilked.*
48 BY . . . END *"To judge by the latter part of his speech."* Volpone was brought in halfway through Voltore's performance.
50 DRAW . . . HEADS *gather his material into topics.* AGGRAVATE *emphasize.*
51 VEHEMENT FIGURES *powerful rhetorical tropes.*
52 SHIFT A SHIRT *so violent were the actions Voltore used to accompany his speech that Mosca humorously compares him to a man trying to change a shirt; or perhaps he means that Voltore worked up such a sweat that he needed to change his shirt.*
54 ANSWER *repay.*

Act V Scene ii

Mosca.　　　　Good, sir.
Volpone.　　　　　　Call the dwarf
And eunuch forth.
Mosca.　　　　Castrone! Nano!
　　　　　　[Enter Castrone and Nano.]
Nano.　　　　　　　　Here.
Volpone. Shall we have a jig now?
Mosca.　　　　　　What you please, sir.
Volpone.　　　　　　　　　Go,
60 Straight give out about the streets, you two,
That I am dead; do it with constancy,
Sadly, do you hear? Impute it to the grief
Of this late slander.　　　[Exeunt Castrone and Nano.]
Mosca.　　　What do you mean, sir?
Volpone.
I shall have instantly my vulture, crow,
65 Raven, come flying hither on the news
To peck for carrion, my she-wolf and all,
Greedy and full of expectation—
Mosca. And then to have it ravished from their mouths?
Volpone. 'Tis true. I will ha' thee put on a gown,
70 And take upon thee as thou wert mine heir;
Show 'em a will. Open that chest and reach
Forth one of those that has the blanks. I'll straight
Put in thy name.
Mosca.　　　It will be rare, sir.
Volpone.　　　　　　　Ay,
When they e'en gape, and find themselves deluded—

59 JIG literally a dance, but a trick is meant. N.
60 STRAIGHT at once.
61 WITH CONSTANCY firmly, i.e. seriously.
62 SADLY gravely.
70 TAKE . . . THEE assume such manners and airs.

Mosca. Yes.

Volpone.   And thou use them scurvily! Dispatch,   75
Get on thy gown.

Mosca.   But what, sir, if they ask
After the body?

Volpone.   Say it was corrupted.

Mosca. I'll say it stunk, sir; and was fain t' have it
Coffined up instantly and sent away.

Volpone. Anything, what thou wilt. Hold, here's my will.   80
Get thee a cap, a count-book, pen and ink,
Papers afore thee; sit as thou wert taking
An inventory of parcels. I'll get up
Behind the curtain, on a stool, and hearken;
Sometime peep over, see how they do look,   85
With what degrees their blood doth leave their faces.
O, 'twill afford me a rare meal of laughter!

Mosca. Your advocate will turn stark dull upon it.

Volpone. It will take off his oratory's edge.

Mosca. But your *clarissimo*, old round-back, he   90
Will crump you like a hog-louse with the touch.

Volpone. And what Corvino?

Mosca.   O sir, look for him
Tomorrow morning with a rope and dagger
To visit all the streets; he must run mad.
My lady too, that came into the court   95

75 DISPATCH *hurry.*
78 WAS FAIN *it was necessary.*
81 COUNT-BOOK *ledger.*
83 PARCELS *parts (of his possessions).*
84 CURTAIN *N.*
90 CLARISSIMO *Venetian of high rank.* ROUND-BACK *i.e. Corbaccio, who obviously stoops.*
91 CRUMP YOU *curl up.*
93 ROPE AND DAGGER *N.*

To bear false witness for your worship—
  Volpone.   Yes,
And kissed me 'fore the fathers, when my face
Flowed all with oils—
  Mosca.   And sweat, sir. Why, your gold
Is such another med'cine, it dries up
100 All those offensive savors! It transforms
The most deformèd, and restores 'em lovely
As 'twere the strange poetical girdle. Jove   *Cestus.*
Could not invent t' himself a shroud more subtle
To pass Acrisius' guards. It is the thing
105 Makes all the world her grace, her youth, her beauty.
  Volpone. I think she loves me.
  Mosca.   Who? The lady, sir?
She's jealous of you.
  Volpone.   Dost thou say so? [*Knocking without.*]
  Mosca.   Hark,
There's some already.
  Volpone.   Look!
  Mosca. [*Peering out.*]   It is the vulture;
He has the quickest scent.
  Volpone.   I'll to my place,
110 Thou to thy posture.
  Mosca.   I am set.
  Volpone.   But Mosca,
Play the artificer now, torture 'em rarely.

---

98 SWEAT *Mosca will not allow Volpone to forget that he was nervous at the trial.*
102 GIRDLE . . . CESTUS *N.*
102–4 JOVE . . . GUARDS *Acrisius was the father of Danaë whom Jove visited in the form of a shower of gold.*
110 POSTURE *pretense, act.*
111 ARTIFICER *player(?), maker of schemes.*

Act V Scene iii

      [Enter Voltore.]
Voltore. How now, my Mosca?
Mosca. *[Writing.]*   Turkey carpets, nine—
Voltore. Taking an inventory? That is well.
Mosca. Two suits of bedding, tissue—
Voltore.   Where's the will?
Let me read that the while.
    [Enter bearers carrying Corbaccio in a chair.]
 Corbaccio.   So, set me down,
And get you home.   *[Exeunt bearers.]*
 Voltore.   Is he come now, to trouble us?   5
Mosca. Of cloth of gold, two more—
Corbaccio.   Is it done, Mosca?
Mosca. Of several vellets, eight—
Voltore.   I like his care.
Corbaccio. Dost thou not hear?
    [Enter Corvino.]
 Corvino.   Ha! Is the hour come, Mosca?
Volpone. *[Aside.]* Ay, now they muster.
       Peeps from behind a traverse.
 Corvino.   What does the advocate here,
Or this Corbaccio?
 Corbaccio.   What do these here?
    [Enter Lady Wouldbe.]
 Lady Wouldbe.   Mosca!   10

1 TURKEY CARPETS *used during this period as table covers.*
3 SUITS *sets.* BEDDING *covers, hangings.* TISSUE *woven gold cloth.*
4 THE WHILE *during the time (the inventory continues).*
7 SEVERAL VELLETS *separate velvet hangings.*
9 TRAVERSE *see* N. *to* V.2.84.

Is his thread spun?

Mosca.　　　　　Eight chests of linen—

Volpone.　　　　　　　　[*Aside.*] O,

My fine Dame Wouldbe, too!

Corvino.　　　　　　Mosca, the will,

That I may show it these and rid 'em hence.

　　Mosca. Six chests of diaper, four of damask—There.

　　　　　[*Gives them the will and continues to write.*]

15　*Corbaccio.* Is that the will?

Mosca.　　　　　　Down-beds, and bolsters—

Volpone.　　　　　　　　[*Aside.*] Rare!

Be busy still. Now they begin to flutter;

They never think of me. Look, see, see, see!

How their swift eyes run over the long deed

Unto the name, and to the legacies,

20 What is bequeathed them there.

　　Mosca.　　　　　Ten suits of hangings—

Volpone. [*Aside.*] Ay, i' their garters, Mosca. Now their hopes

Are at the gasp.

　　Voltore.　　Mosca the heir!

　　Corbaccio.　　　　　What's that?

Volpone. [*Aside.*] My advocate is dumb; look to my merchant.

He has heard of some strange storm, a ship is lost,

25 He faints; my lady will swoon. Old glazen-eyes

He hath not reached his despair, yet.

　　Corbaccio.　　　　　All these

Are out of hope; I'm sure the man.

　　Corvino.　　　　　But, Mosca—

Mosca. Two cabinets—

11 THREAD SPUN *N.*

14 DIAPER *cloth woven with reiterated pattern.*

20–1 HANGINGS . . . GARTERS *"Hang themselves in their own garters," a mocking
　　formula for suicide.*

22 GASP *last gasp.*

Corvino.   Is this in earnest?

Mosca.   One
Of ebony—

Corvino. Or do you but delude me?

Mosca. The other, mother of pearl—I am very busy.   30
Good faith, it is a fortune thrown upon me—
Item, one salt of agate—not my seeking.

Lady Wouldbe. Do you hear, sir?

Mosca.   A perfumed box—Pray you forbear,
You see I'm troubled—made of an onyx—

Lady Wouldbe.   How?

Mosca. Tomorrow, or next day, I shall be at leisure   35
To talk with you all.

Corvino.   Is this my large hope's issue?

Lady Wouldbe. Sir, I must have a fairer answer.

Mosca.   Madam!
Marry, and shall: pray you, fairly quit my house.
Nay, raise no tempest with your looks; but hark you,
Remember what your ladyship offered me   40
To put you in an heir; go to, think on 't.
And what you said e'en your best madams did
For maintenance, and why not you? Enough.
Go home and use the poor Sir Pol, your knight, well,
For fear I tell some riddles. Go, be melancholic.   45

                         [*Exit Lady Wouldbe.*]

Volpone. [*Aside.*] O my fine devil!

Corvino.   Mosca, pray you a word.

Mosca. Lord! Will not you take your dispatch hence yet?

32 SALT *saltcellar.*

38 FAIRLY *this word has roughly the present-day sense of "just" in "just leave the house."*

40 REMEMBER . . . ME *Lady Wouldbe has obviously offered her favors to Mosca. This fact explains the tone of line IV.6.101.*

47 DISPATCH *dismissal.*

Methinks of all you should have been th' example.
Why should you stay here? With what thought? What promise?
50 Hear you: do not you know I know you an ass,
And that you would most fain have been a wittol
If fortune would have let you? That you are
A declared cuckold, on good terms? This pearl,   [*Holding*
You'll say, was yours? Right. This diamond?   *up jewels.*]
55 I'll not deny't, but thank you. Much here else?
It may be so. Why, think that these good works
May help to hide your bad. I'll not betray you,
Although you be but extraordinary,
And have it only in title, it sufficeth.
60 Go home, be melancholic too, or mad.   [*Exit Corvino.*]
   Volpone. [*Aside.*] Rare, Mosca! How his villainy becomes him!
   Voltore. Certain he doth delude all these for me.
   Corbaccio. Mosca the heir?   [*Still straining to read the will.*]
   Volpone.   [*Aside.*] O, his four eyes have found it!
   Corbaccio. I'm cozened, cheated, by a parasite slave!
65 Harlot, th'ast gulled me.
   Mosca.   Yes, sir. Stop your mouth,
Or I shall draw the only tooth is left.
Are not you he, that filthy, covetous wretch
With the three legs, that here, in hope of prey,
Have, any time this three year, snuffed about
70 With your most grov'ling nose, and would have hired

---

48 EXAMPLE *i.e. by leaving first show the others the way.*
51 WITTOL *knowing cuckold.*
55 ELSE *otherwise.*
58–9 ALTHOUGH . . . SUFFICETH "*Although you are an unusual cuckold, being one in title but not in fact, this will do for you.*"
65 HARLOT *malicious fellow—originally applied to men.*
68 THREE LEGS *Corbaccio uses a cane.*
69 ANY TIME *at any time.*

Me to the pois'ning of my patron, sir?
Are not you he that have, today, in court,
Professed the disinheriting of your son?
Perjured yourself? Go home, and die, and stink.
If you but croak a syllable, all comes out.   75
Away, and call your porters! Go, go, stink.   [*Exit Corbaccio.*]
   Volpone. [*Aside.*] Excellent varlet!
   Voltore.   Now, my faithful Mosca,
I find thy constancy.
   Mosca.   Sir?
   Voltore.   Sincere.
   Mosca.   A table
Of porphyry—I mar'l you'll be thus troublesome.
   Voltore. Nay, leave off now, they are gone.
   Mosca.   Why, who are you?   80
What! Who did send for you? O, cry you mercy,
Reverend sir! Good faith, I am grieved for you,
That any chance of mine should thus defeat
Your—I must needs say—most deserving travails.
But I protest, sir, it was cast upon me,   85
And I could, almost, wish to be without it,
But that the will o' th' dead must be observed.
Marry, my joy is that you need it not;
You have a gift, sir—thank your education—
Will never let you want while there are men   90
And malice to breed causes. Would I had
But half the like, for all my fortune, sir.
If I have any suits—as I do hope,
Things being so easy and direct, I shall not—

79 MAR'L *marvel.*
81 CRY YOU MERCY *beg your pardon.*
83 CHANCE *luck.*
91 CAUSES *lawsuits.*
94 THINGS . . . DIRECT *i.e. the will being so clear and uncomplicated.*

95 I will make bold with your obstreperous aid;
   Conceive me, for your fee, sir. In meantime,
   You that have so much law, I know ha' the conscience
   Not to be covetous of what is mine.
   Good sir, I thank you for my plate; 'twill help
100 To set up a young man. Good faith, you look
   As you were costive; best go home and purge, sir. [*Exit Voltore.*]
    Volpone. Bid him eat lettuce well! My witty mischief,
                  [*Coming from behind curtain.*]
   Let me embrace thee. O that I could now
   Transform thee to a Venus—Mosca, go,
105 Straight take my habit of *clarissimo*,
   And walk the streets; be seen, torment 'em more.
   We must pursue as well as plot. Who would
   Have lost this feast?
    Mosca.   I doubt it will lose them.
    Volpone. O, my recovery shall recover all.
110 That I could now but think on some disguise
   To meet 'em in, and ask 'em questions.
   How I would vex 'em still at every turn!
    Mosca. Sir, I can fit you.
    Volpone.   Canst thou?
    Mosca.   Yes, I know
   One o' th' *commendatori*, sir, so like you;

95 OBSTREPEROUS *clamorous.*
96 CONCEIVE *understand.* FOR YOUR FEE *i.e. "I will not ask your services gratis but will pay the standard price."*
97 HAVE *know.*
99 PLATE *the one Voltore gave earlier as a present.*
101 COSTIVE *constipated.*
102 LETTUCE *a laxative.*
105 HABIT *robe. Special dress was decreed for various social orders.*
108 LOSE *get rid of.*
113 FIT YOU *"find just what you want."*
114 COMMENDATORI *sergeants, or minor officials, of the court.*

Him will I straight make drunk, and bring you his habit.   115
   Volpone. A rare disguise, and answering thy brain!
O, I will be a sharp disease unto 'em.
   Mosca. Sir, you must look for curses—
   Volpone.   Till they burst;
The fox fares ever best when he is cursed.   *[Exeunt.]*

116 ANSWERING *resembling (the rareness of Mosca's brain).*
117 SHARP *painful.*
119 *A proverbial saying.*

Act V Scene iv

[*Sir Politic's house.*]
[*Enter Peregrine disguised, and three Merchants.*]
   Peregrine. Am I enough disguised?
   1st Merchant.   I warrant you.
   Peregrine. All my ambition is to fright him only.
   2nd Merchant. If you could ship him away, 'twere excellent.
   3rd Merchant. To Zant, or to Aleppo?
   Peregrine.   Yes, and ha' his
Adventures put i' th' book of voyages,   5
And his gulled story registered for truth?
Well, gentlemen, when I am in a while,
And that you think us warm in our discourse,
Know your approaches.
   1st Merchant.   Trust it to our care. *[Exeunt Merchants.]*
                   [Enter Woman.]

1 WARRANT *assure.*
4 ZANT *one of the Ionian islands.*
5 BOOK OF VOYAGES *popular collections of foreign voyages such as Hakluyt's.*
9 KNOW . . . APPROACHES "*Come in at the right time.*"

10   *Peregrine.* Save you, fair lady. Is Sir Pol within?
       Woman. I do not know, sir.
       Peregrine.   Pray you say unto him,
       Here is a merchant, upon earnest business,
       Desires to speak with him.
       Woman.   I will see, sir.
       Peregrine.   Pray you. [*Exit Woman.*]
       I see the family is all female here.
                     [*Re-enter Woman.*]
15   *Woman.* He says, sir, he has weighty affairs of state
       That now require him whole; some other time
       You may possess him.
       Peregrine.   Pray you, say again,
       If those require him whole, these will exact him,
       Whereof I bring him tidings. [*Exit Woman.*] What might be
20   His grave affair of state now? How to make
       Bolognian sausages here in Venice, sparing
       One o' th' ingredients?
                   [*Re-enter Woman.*]
       Woman.   Sir, he says he knows
       By your word "tidings" that you are no statesman,
       And therefore wills you stay.
       Peregrine.   Sweet, pray you return him:
25   I have not read so many proclamations
       And studied them for words, as he has done,
       But—Here he deigns to come.
                   [*Enter Sir Politic.*]

16 REQUIRE HIM WHOLE *occupy his entire attention.*
17 POSSESS *Sir Pol's elaborate way of saying "see."*
18 EXACT *force.*
21 SPARING *leaving out.*
23 TIDINGS *"intelligences" would be the statesman's word.*
24 RETURN HIM *"say to him in return."*

   Sir Politic.   Sir, I must crave
Your courteous pardon. There hath chanced today
Unkind disaster 'twixt my lady and me,
And I was penning my apology   30
To give her satisfaction, as you came now.
   Peregrine. Sir, I am grieved I bring you worse disaster:
The gentleman you met at th' port today,
That told you he was newly arrived—
   Sir Politic.   Ay, was
A fugitive punk?
   Peregrine.   No, sir, a spy set on you,   35
And he has made relation to the Senate
That you professed to him to have a plot
To sell the state of Venice to the Turk.
   Sir Politic. O me!
   Peregrine.   For which warrants are signed by this time
To apprehend you and to search your study   40
For papers—
   Sir Politic. Alas, sir, I have none but notes
Drawn out of play-books—
   Peregrine.   All the better, sir.
   Sir Politic. And some essays. What shall I do?
   Peregrine.   Sir, best
Convey yourself into a sugar-chest,
Or, if you could lie round, a frail were rare,   45
And I could send you aboard.
   Sir Politic.   Sir, I but talked so
For discourse' sake merely. *They knock without.*
   Peregrine.   Hark, they are there.

35 PUNK *prostitute.*
42 PLAY-BOOKS *printed plays.*
45 FRAIL *rush basket used for packing figs.*
47 DISCOURSE' *conversation's.*

    Sir Politic. I am a wretch, a wretch!

    Peregrine.   What will you do, sir?

Ha' you ne'er a currant-butt to leap into?

50 They'll put you to the rack, you must be sudden.

    Sir Politic. Sir, I have an engine—

    3rd Merchant. [*Calling from off-stage.*] Sir Politic Wouldbe!

    2nd Merchant. Where is he?

    Sir Politic.   That I have thought upon beforetime.

    Peregrine. What is it?

    Sir Politic.   I shall ne'er endure the torture!

Marry, it is, sir, of a tortoise-shell,

55 Fitted for these extremities. Pray you, sir, help me. [*He gets into*

Here I've a place, sir, to put back my legs;   *a large*

Please you to lay it on, sir. With this cap   *tortoise shell.*]

And my black gloves, I'll lie, sir, like a tortoise,

Till they are gone.

    Peregrine.   And call you this an engine?

60   *Sir Politic.* Mine own device—Good sir, bid my wife's women

To burn my papers.

               They [*The three Merchants*] *rush in.*

    1st Merchant.   Where's he hid?

    3rd Merchant.   We must,

And will, sure, find him.

    2nd Merchant.   Which is his study?

    1st Merchant.   What

Are you, sir?

    Peregrine. I'm a merchant that came here

To look upon this tortoise.

---

49 CURRANT-BUTT *cask for currants.*

51 ENGINE *device.*

55 FITTED *the Quarto reads " apted," i.e. suited.*

57 IT *i.e. the shell.*

3rd Merchant.   How!

1st Merchant.   St. Mark!
What beast is this?

Peregrine.   It is a fish.

2nd Merchant. [*Striking the tortoise.*] Come out here!   65

Peregrine. Nay, you may strike him, sir, and tread upon him.
He'll bear a cart.

1st Merchant. What, to run over him?

Peregrine.   Yes.

3rd Merchant. Let's jump upon him.

2nd Merchant.   Can he not go?

Peregrine.   He creeps, sir.

1st Merchant. Let's see him creep. [*Prodding him.*]

   Peregrine.   No, good sir, you will hurt him.

2nd Merchant. Heart, I'll see him creep, or prick his guts.   70

3rd Merchant. Come out here!

Peregrine. [*Aside to Sir Politic.*] Pray you, sir, creep a little.

1st Merchant.   Forth!

2nd Merchant. Yet further.

Peregrine. [*Aside to Sir Politic.*] Good sir, creep.

2nd Merchant.   We'll see his legs.

      They pull off the shell and discover him.

3rd Merchant. Godso, he has garters!

1st Merchant.   Ay, and gloves!

2nd Merchant.   Is this
Your fearful tortoise?

   Peregrine.   Now, Sir Pol, we are even.   [*Throwing*
For your next project I shall be prepared.   *off his*   75
I am sorry for the funeral of your notes, sir.   *disguise.*]

68 GO *walk.*

70 HEART *a mild oath.*

SD DISCOVER *disclose.*

76 FUNERAL *burning. The ironic comparison is to a funeral pyre.*

1st Merchant. 'Twere a rare motion to be seen in Fleet Street.
2nd Merchant. Ay, i' the term.
1st Merchant.   Or Smithfield, in the fair.
3rd Merchant. Methinks 'tis but a melancholic sight.

80 *Peregrine.* Farewell, most politic tortoise!

> [*Exeunt Peregrine and Merchants.*]

Sir Politic.   Where's my lady?
Knows she of this?
Woman.   I know not, sir.
Sir Politic.   Inquire.   [*Exit Woman.*]
O, I shall be the fable of all feasts,
The freight of the *gazetti*, ship-boys' tale,
And, which is worst, even talk for ordinaries.

> [*Re-enter Woman.*]

85 *Woman.* My lady's come most melancholic home,
And says, sir, she will straight to sea, for physic.
Sir Politic. And I, to shun this place and clime forever,
Creeping with house on back, and think it well
To shrink my poor head in my politic shell.   [*Exeunt.*]

---

77 MOTION *puppet show.*
78 TERM *the period when the courts were in session and London filled with
      people.* SMITHFIELD . . . FAIR *Bartholomew Fair, with many sideshows, was
      held in Smithfield.*
83 FREIGHT *topic.* GAZETTI *newspapers.*
84 ORDINARIES *taverns.*
86 STRAIGHT . . . SEA *sail at once.* FOR PHYSIC *for health.*

Act V Scene v

                    [Volpone's house.]
        [Enter Volpone in the habit of a commendatore,
                  Mosca of a clarissimo.]

Volpone. Am I then like him?

Mosca.   O sir, you are he;

No man can sever you.

Volpone.   Good.

Mosca.   But what am I?

Volpone. 'Fore heav'n, a brave *clarissimo*, thou becom'st it!

Pity thou wert not born one.

Mosca.   If I hold

My made one, 'twill be well.

Volpone.   I'll go and see   5

What news, first, at the court   *[Exit.]*

Mosca.   Do so. My fox

Is out on his hole, and ere he shall re-enter,

I'll make him languish in his borrowed case,

Except he come to composition with me.

Androgyno, Castrone, Nano! *[Enter Androgyno, Castrone, and*

All.   Here.   *Nano.]* 10

  Mosca. Go recreate yourselves abroad, go sport.   *[Exeunt*

So, now I have the keys and am possessed.   *the three.]*

1 HIM *i.e. the* commendatore.

2 SEVER *separate, distinguish.*

4 HOLD *retain.*

5 MADE ONE *assumed status (of clarissimo).*

6–7 FOX . . . HOLE *N.*

7 ON *of.*

8 CASE *disguise.*

9 EXCEPT *unless.* COMPOSITION *agreement.*

11 RECREATE *enjoy.*

12 POSSESSED *in possession.*

Since he will needs be dead afore his time,
I'll bury him, or gain by him. I'm his heir,
15 And so will keep me, till he share at least.
To cozen him of all were but a cheat
Well placed; no man would cònstrue it a sin.
Let his sport pay for 't. This is called the fox-trap.   [*Exit.*]

13 WILL NEEDS BE *insists on being.*
15 KEEP ME *remain.*
18 LET . . . IT "*Let the pleasure he is getting from all this pay him for what it is going to cost.*"

Act V Scene vi

[*A Venetian street.*]
[*Enter Corbaccio and Corvino.*]
Corbaccio. They say the court is set.
Corvino.   We must maintain
Our first tale good, for both our reputations.
Corbaccio. Why, mine's no tale! My son would, there, have killed me.
Corvino. That's true, I had forgot. Mine is, I am sure.
5 But for your will, sir.
Corbaccio.   Ay, I'll come upon him
For that hereafter, now his patron's dead.   [*Enter Volpone in*
Volpone. Signor Corvino! And Corbaccio! Sir,   *disguise.*]
Much joy unto you.
Corvino.   Of what?
Volpone.   The sudden good
Dropped down upon you—
Corbaccio.   Where?
Volpone.   And none knows how,
From old Volpone, sir.

1-2 MAINTAIN . . . GOOD "*continue to insist on the truth of the tales told first in court.*"
5 HIM *i.e. Mosca.*

Corbaccio.　　　　Out, arrant knave!　　　　　　　　　10
Volpone. Let not your too much wealth, sir, make you furious.
Corbaccio. Away, thou varlet.
Volpone.　　　　　　Why, sir?
Corbaccio.　　　　　　　　Dost thou mock me?
Volpone. You mock the world, sir; did you not change wills?
Corbaccio. Out, harlot!
Volpone.　　　　　O! Belike you are the man,
Signor Corvino? Faith, you carry it well;　　　　　　　15
You grow not mad withal. I love your spirit.
You are not over-leavened with your fortune.
You should ha' some would swell now like a wine-fat
With such an autumn—Did he gi' you all, sir?
　Corvino. Avoid, you rascal.
　Volpone.　　　　　Troth, your wife has shown　20
Herself a very woman! But you are well,
You need not care, you have a good estate
To bear it out, sir, better by this chance.
Except Corbaccio have a share?
　Corbaccio.　　　　　Hence, varlet.
　Volpone. You will not be a'known, sir? Why, 'tis wise.　25
Thus do all gamesters, at all games, dissemble.
No man will seem to win.　　[*Exeunt Corvino and Corbaccio.*]
　　　　　　　Here comes my vulture,
Heaving his beak up i' the air, and snuffing.

12 VARLET *low fellow; also the title for a sergeant of the court.*
13 CHANGE *exchange.*
17 OVER-LEAVENED *puffed up.*
18 FAT *vat.*
19 AUTUMN *i.e. rich harvest.*
20 AVOID *get out!*
21 VERY *true.*
23 BEAR IT OUT *carry it off.*
24 EXCEPT *unless.*
25 A'KNOWN *acknowledged (the heir).*

Act V Scene vii

[*Enter Voltore to Volpone.*]

Voltore. Outstripped thus, by a parasite! A slave,
Would run on errands, and make legs for crumbs?
Well, what I'll do—
    Volpone.   The court stays for your worship.
I e'en rejoice, sir, at your worship's happiness,
5 And that it fell into so learned hands,
That understand the fingering—
    Voltore.   What do you mean?
    Volpone. I mean to be a suitor to your worship
For the small tenement, out of reparations,
That at the end of your long row of houses,
10 By the *Pescheria*; it was, in Volpone's time,
Your predecessor, ere he grew diseased,
A handsome, pretty, customed bawdy-house
As any was in Venice—none dispraised—
But fell with him. His body and that house
15 Decayed together.
    Voltore.   Come, sir, leave your prating.
    Volpone. Why, if your worship give me but your hand,
That I may ha' the refusal, I have done.

1 OUTSTRIPPED *outrun, beaten.*
2 WOULD "*who used to.*" LEGS *bows.*
8 REPARATIONS *repairs.*
10 PESCHERIA *fish-market.*
12 CUSTOMED *well patronized.*
13 NONE DISPRAISED "*not to say anything bad of the others.*"
17 REFUSAL *option.* HAVE DONE *am finished (asking favors).*

'Tis a mere toy to you, sir, candle-rents.
As your learned worship knows—

    Voltore.   What do I know?

    Volpone. Marry, no end of your wealth, sir, God decrease it.   20

    Voltore. Mistaking knave! What, mock'st thou my misfortune?

    Volpone. His blessing on your heart, sir; would 'twere more!

                              [Exit Voltore.]

Now, to my first again, at the next corner.

18 TOY *trifle.* CANDLE-RENTS *rents from slums.*
20 DECREASE *an intentional malapropism—he pretends to mean "increase."*

Act V Scene viii

[Volpone remains on stage to one side. Corbaccio and Corvino enter.]
        [Mosca passes slowly across stage.]

    Corbaccio. See, in our habit! See the impudent varlet!

    Corvino. That I could shoot mine eyes at him, like gunstones!

                             [Exit Mosca.]

    Volpone. But is this true, sir, of the parasite?

    Corbaccio. Again t' afflict us? Monster!

    Volpone.   In good faith, sir,
I'm heartily grieved a beard of your grave length   5
Should be so over-reached. I never brooked
That parasite's hair; methought his nose should cozen.
There still was somewhat in his look did promise
The bane of a *clarissimo.*

    Corbaccio.   Knave—

1 OUR HABIT *i.e. the dress of a clarissimo.*
2 GUNSTONES *stone cannonballs.*
5 BEARD . . . LENGTH *man as old and wise as you.*
6 OVER-REACHED *outsmarted.* BROOKED *could endure.*
8 STILL *always.* SOMEWHAT *something.*

Act V Scene viii

    Volpone.   <u>Methinks</u>
10 <u>Yet you, that are so traded i' the world,</u>
    <u>A witty merchant, the fine bird Corvino,</u>
    <u>That have such moral emblems on your name,</u>
    <u>Should not have sung your shame, and dropped your cheese,</u>
    <u>To let the fox laugh at your emptiness.</u>
15   *Corvino.* Sirrah, you think the privilege of the place,
    And your red, saucy cap, that seems to me
    Nailed to your jolt-head with those two chequins,
    Can warrant your abuses. Come you hither:
    You shall perceive, sir, I dare beat you. Approach.
20   *Volpone.* No haste, sir. I do know your valor well,
    Since you durst publish what you are, sir.
    Corvino.   Tarry,
    I'd speak with you.
    Volpone.   Sir, sir, another time— [*Backing away.*]
    Corvino. Nay, now.
    Volpone.   O God, sir! I were a wise man
    Would stand the fury of a distracted cuckold. *Mosca walks by 'em.*
25   *Corbaccio.* What, come again!
    Volpone.   [*Aside.*] Upon 'em, Mosca; save me.
    Corbaccio. The air's infected where he breathes.
    Corvino.   Let's fly him.
               [*Exeunt Corvino and Corbaccio.*]
    Volpone. Excellent basilisk! Turn upon the vulture.

10 TRADED *experienced.*
12–14 MORAL . . . EMPTINESS N.
15 PRIVILEGE . . . PLACE "*the immunity conferred by your rank.*"
16–17 CAP . . . CHEQUINS *a commendatore wore a red hat with two gilt buttons*
    on the front.
17 JOLT-HEAD *blockhead.*
18 WARRANT *sanction.*
21 WHAT YOU ARE *i.e. a cuckold.*
24 WOULD "*if I would.*" STAND *oppose.*
27 BASILISK *a serpent believed to be able to kill with its glance.*

Act V Scene ix

[*Enter Voltore.*]

Voltore. Well, flesh-fly, it is summer with you now;
Your winter will come on.

Mosca.   Good advocate,
Pray thee not rail, nor threaten out of place thus;
Thou'lt make a solecism, as Madam says.
Get you a biggen more; your brain breaks loose.   [*Exit.*]   5

Voltore. Well, sir.

Volpone.   Would you ha' me beat the insolent slave?
Throw dirt upon his first good clothes?

Voltore.   This same
Is doubtless some familiar!

Volpone.   Sir, the court,
In troth, stays for you. I am mad; a mule
That never read Justinian, should get up   10
And ride an advocate! Had you no quirk
To avoid gullage, sir, by such a creature?
I hope you do but jest; he has not done 't;
This's but confederacy to blind the rest.
You are the heir?

1 FLESH-FLY *the meaning of "Mosca."*
4 MADAM *i.e. Lady Wouldbe. See IV.2.43.*
5 BIGGEN *lawyer's cap.* MORE *i.e. to add to the one you have.*
7 THIS SAME *i.e. Volpone.*
8 FAMILIAR *evil spirit.*
9 I AM MAD *"it is madness" (to believe that this has happened).*
10 JUSTINIAN *Roman legal code assembled at the order of the Emperor Justinian.*
11 QUIRK *device.*
12 GULLAGE *being gulled, fooled.*
14 CONFEDERACY *an agreement (between Voltore and Mosca).*

   Voltore.   A strange, officious,
Troublesome knave! Thou dost torment me.
   Volpone.   *[Aside.]* —I know—
It cannot be, sir, that you should be cozened;
'Tis not within the wit of man to do it.
You are so wise, so prudent, and 'tis fit
20 That wealth and wisdom still should to together.   *[Exeunt.]*

Act V Scene x

                  [The Scrutineo.]
  [Enter four Avocatori, Notario, Commendatori, Bonario, Celia,
                Corbaccio, Corvino.]
   1st Avocatore. Are all the parties here?
   Notario.   All but the advocate.
   2nd Avocatore. And here he comes.
        [Enter Voltore, Volpone following him.]
   Avocatori.   Then bring 'em forth to sentence.
   Voltore. O my most honored fathers, let your mercy
Once win upon your justice, to forgive—
5 I am distracted—
   Volpone. [Aside.] What will he do now?
   Voltore.   O,
I know not which t' address myself to first,
Whether your fatherhoods, or these innocents—
   Corvino. [Aside.] Will he betray himself?
   Voltore.   Whom equally
I have abused, out of most covetous ends—

2 AVOCATORI *N.* 'EM *i.e. Celia and Bonario.*
4 WIN UPON *overcome.*
9 OUT . . . ENDS *because of covetous desires.*

Corvino. The man is mad!

Corbaccio.   What's that?

Corvino.   He is possessed.   10

Voltore. For which, now struck in conscience, here I prostrate
Myself at your offended feet, for pardon. [*He kneels.*]

1st, 2nd Avocatori. Arise.

Celia.   O heav'n, how just thou art!

Volpone.   [*Aside.*] I'm caught
I' mine own noose.

Corvino. [*Aside to Corbaccio.*] Be constant, sir, nought now
Can help but impudence.

1st Avocatore.   Speak forward.

Commendatore. [*To the Courtroom.*]   Silence!   15

Voltore. It is not passion in me, reverend fathers,
But only conscience, conscience, my good sires,
That makes me now tell truth. That parasite,
That knave, hath been the instrument of all.

Avocatori. Where is that knave? Fetch him.

Volpone.   I go.   [*Exit.*]

Corvino.   Grave fathers,   20
This man's distracted, he confessed it now,
For, hoping to be old Volpone's heir,
Who now is dead—

3rd Avocatore.   How!

2nd Avocatore.   Is Volpone dead?

Corvino. Dead since, grave fathers—

Bonario.   O sure vengeance!

1st Avocatore.   Stay.
Then he was no deceiver.   25

10 POSSESSED *in the possession of the devil.*
14 CONSTANT *"continue firm" (in your story).*
15 IMPUDENCE *Latin* impudens, *shameless.* FORWARD *on.*
19 INSTRUMENT OF ALL *arranger of everything.*
21 DISTRACTED *out of his wits—see line 5 above.*

191

Act V Scene x

    Voltore.   O, no, none;
The parasite, grave fathers.
    Corvino.   He does speak
Out of mere envy, 'cause the servant's made
The thing he gaped for. Please your fatherhoods,
This is the truth; though I'll not justify
30 The other, but he may be some-deal faulty.
    Voltore. Ay, to your hopes, as well as mine, Corvino.
But I'll use modesty. Pleaseth your wisdoms
To view these certain notes, and but confer them;
                          [*Gives them notes.*]
As I hope favor, they shall speak clear truth.
35   *Corvino.* The devil has entered him!
    Bonario.   Or bides in you.
    4th Avocatore. We have done ill, by a public officer
To send for him, if he be heir.
    2nd Avocatore.   For whom?
    4th Avocatore. Him that they call the parasite.
    3rd Avocatore.   'Tis true,
He is a man of great estate now left.
40   *4th Avocatore.* Go you, and learn his name, and say the court
Entreats his presence here, but to the clearing
Of some few doubts.   [*Exit Notario.*]
    2nd Avocatore. This same's a labyrinth!
    1st Avocatore. Stand you unto your first report?

30 SOME-DEAL *somewhat.* Quarto reads "somewhere."
32 MODESTY *restraint.*
33 CERTAIN *particular.* CONFER *compare.*
35 DEVIL . . . HIM *N.* BIDES *abides, dwells.*
36–7 WE . . . HEIR *Mosca's new dignity entitles him to a ceremonious invitation, not a rude summons.*
41 BUT TO *only for.*
42 DOUBTS *questions.*

192

Corvino.   My state,
My life, my fame—
    Bonario.   Where is't?
    Corvino.   Are at the stake.
    1st Avocatore. Is yours so too?
    Corbaccio.   The advocate's a knave,   45
And has a forkèd tongue—
    2nd Avocatore.   Speak to the point.
    Corbaccio. So is the parasite too.
    1st Avocatore.   This is confusion.
    Voltore. I do beseech your fatherhoods, read but those.
    Corvino. And credit nothing the false spirit hath writ.
It cannot be but he is possessed, grave fathers.   50

48 THOSE *i.e. the notes he has given them.*
49 CREDIT *believe.*

Act V Scene xi

                 [*A street. Volpone alone.*]
    Volpone. To make a snare for mine own neck! And run
My head into it wilfully, with laughter!
When I had newly 'scaped, was free and clear!
Out of mere wantonness! O, the dull devil
Was in this brain of mine when I devised it,   5
And Mosca gave it second; he must now
Help to sear up this vein, or we bleed dead.
        [*Enter Nano, Androgyno, and Castrone.*]
How now! Who let you loose? Whither go you now?

4 WANTONNESS *playfulness.*
6 GAVE IT SECOND *seconded the idea.*
7 SEAR *treat with a hot iron—one method for closing cut veins.*

What, to buy gingerbread, or to drown kitlings?

10   *Nano.* Sir, Master Mosca called us out of doors,
And bid us all go play, and took the keys.
    Androgyno.   Yes.
    Volpone. Did Master Mosca take the keys? Why, so!
I am farther in. These are my fine conceits!
I must be merry, with a mischief to me!

15 What a vile wretch was I, that could not bear
My fortune soberly; I must ha' my crotchets
And my conundrums! Well, go you and seek him.
His meaning may be truer than my fear.
Bid him, he straight come to me to the court;

20 Thither will I, and if't be possible,
Unscrew my advocate, upon new hopes.
When I provoked him, then I lost myself.   [*Exeunt.*]

9 KITLINGS *kittens.*

13 FARTHER IN *deeper in (trouble).* CONCEITS *ideas, plans.*

16 CROTCHETS *fancies, whims.*

17 CONUNDRUMS *puzzles—perhaps a reference to the puzzling of the three disappointed heirs in scenes 6–9.*

18 "*His intentions may be more honest than I fear they are.*"

21 UNSCREW *i.e.* "*get him to change his position again*"—*Voltore is pictured as being as crooked and as retentive as a screw, or perhaps some variety of boring insect.*

Act V Scene xii

[*The Scrutineo.*]·

[*Four Avocatori, Notario, Voltore, Bonario, Celia, Corbaccio, Corvino.*]
    1st Avocatore. [*Looking over Voltore's notes.*] These things can
    ne'er be reconciled. He here
Professeth that the gentleman was wronged,

And that the gentlewoman was brought thither,
Forced by her husband, and there left.

    Voltore.   Most true.

    Celia. How ready is heav'n to those that pray!

    1st Avocatore.   But that   5
Volpone would have ravished her, he holds
Utterly false, knowing his impotence.

    Corvino. Grave fathers, he is possessed; again, I say,
Possessed. Nay, if there be possession
And obsession, he has both.

    3rd Avocatore.   Here comes our officer.   10
                 [*Enter Volpone, still disguised.*]

    Volpone. The parasite will straight be here, grave fathers.

    4th Avocatore. You might invent some other name, sir varlet.

    3rd Avocatore. Did not the notary meet him?

    Volpone.   Not that I know.

    4th Avocatore. His coming will clear all.

    2nd Avocatore.   Yet, it is misty.

    Voltore. May't please your fatherhoods—

    Volpone.   Sir, the parasite   15
              Volpone whispers [*to*] *the Advocate.*
Willed me to tell you that his master lives;
That you are still the man; your hopes the same;
And this was only a jest—

    Voltore.   How?

    Volpone.   Sir, to try
If you were firm, and how you stood affected.

---

 5 READY *available (to help).*

9–10 POSSESSION . . . OBSESSION *see N. to V.10.35.*

12 INVENT *find—because Mosca is now wealthy the term parasite is no longer suitable.*

14 CLEAR *clear up.* MISTY *confused.*

19 STOOD AFFECTED *truly felt(?).*

Act V Scene xii

20   *Voltore.* Art sure he lives?
     Volpone.   Do I live, sir?
     Voltore.   O me!
     I was too violent.
         Volpone.   Sir, you may redeem it:
     They said you were possessed: fall down, and seem so.
     I'll help to make it good. God bless the man!   *Voltore falls.*
              [*Aside to Voltore.*]
     —Stop your wind hard, and swell—See, see, see, see!
25   He vomits crooked pins! His eyes are set
     Like a dead hare's hung in a poulter's shop!
     His mouth's running away! Do you see, signior?
     Now, 'tis in his belly.
         Corvino.   Ay, the devil!
     Volpone. Now, in his throat.
         Corvino.   Ay, I perceive it plain.
30   *Volpone.* 'Twill out, 'twill out! Stand clear. See where it flies!
     In shape of a blue toad, with a bat's wings! [*Pointing.*]
     Do you not see it, sir?
         Corbaccio.   What? I think I do.
     Corvino. 'Tis too manifest.
         Volpone.   Look! He comes t' himself.
     Voltore. Where am I?
         Volpone.   Take good heart, the worst is past, sir.
35   You are dispossessed.
             1st *Avocatore.*   What accident is this?
             2nd *Avocatore.* Sudden, and full of wonder!

     20 DO . . . SIR? *N.*
     24 STOP . . . WIND "*hold your breath.*"
     24–31 *N.*
     26 POULTER'S *poultry seller's.*
     27 RUNNING AWAY *awry and moving wildly.*
     33 COMES T' HIMSELF *revives.*

196

3rd Avocatore.   If he were
Possessed, as it appears, all this is nothing. [*Waving notes.*]

   Corvino. He has been often subject to these fits.

   1st Avocatore. Show him that writing.—Do you know it, sir?

   Volpone. [*Aside.*] Deny it sir, forswear it, know it not.   40

   Voltore. Yes, I do know it well, it is my hand;
But all that it contains is false.

   Bonario.   O practice!

   2nd Avocatore. What maze is this!

   1st Avocatore.   Is he not guilty then,
Whom you, there, name the parasite?

   Voltore.   Grave fathers,
No more than his good patron, old Volpone.   45

   4th Avocatore. Why, he is dead.

   Voltore.   O, no, my honored fathers.
He lives—

   1st Avocatore. How! Lives?

   Voltore.   Lives.

   2nd Avocatore.   This is subtler yet!

   3rd Avocatore. You said he was dead.

   Voltore.   Never.

   3rd Avocatore.   You said so!

   Corvino.   I heard so.

   4th Avocatore. Here comes the gentleman, make him way.
                 [*Enter Mosca.*]

   3rd Avocatore.   A stool!

   4th Avocatore. A proper man and, were Volpone dead,   50
A fit match for my daughter.

   3rd Avocatore.   Give him way.

---

42 PRACTICE *intrigue.*
47 SUBTLER *more intricate.*
49 MAKE HIM WAY "*Open a path for him.*"
50 PROPER *handsome.*

    Volpone. [*Aside to Mosca.*] Mosca, I was almost lost; the advocate

Had betrayed all; but now it is recovered.

All's o' the hinge again. Say I am living.

55   *Mosca.* What busy knave is this? Most reverend fathers,

I sooner had attended your grave pleasures,

But that my order for the funeral

Of my dear patron did require me—

    Volpone.   [*Aside.*] Mosca!

  Mosca. Whom I intend to bury like a gentleman.

60   *Volpone.* [*Aside.*] Ay, quick, and cozen me of all.

    2nd Avocatore.   Still stranger!

More intricate!

    1st Avocatore. And come about again!

    4th Avocatore. [*Aside.*] It is a match, my daughter is bestowed.

    Mosca. [*Aside to Volpone.*] Will you gi' me half?

    Volpone. [*Half aloud.*]   First I'll be hanged.

    Mosca.   [*Aside.*] I know

Your voice is good, cry not so loud.

    1st Avocatore.   Demand

65 The advocate. Sir, did not you affirm

Volpone was alive?

    Volpone.   Yes, and he is;

This gent'man told me so. [*Aside to Mosca.*] Thou shalt have half.

    Mosca. Whose drunkard is this same? Speak, some that know

    him.

53 RECOVERED *N.*

54 O' *on.*

55 BUSY *meddling.*

60 QUICK *alive.*

61 COME . . . AGAIN *reversed once more—i.e. having been declared dead, then living, Volpone is once more dead.*

62 BESTOWED *i.e. in marriage.*

64 DEMAND *question.*

I never saw his face. [*Aside to Volpone.*] I cannot now
Afford it you so cheap.

  Volpone.   [*Aside.*] No?

  1st Avocatore. [*To Voltore.*] What say you?   70

  Voltore. The officer told me.

  Volpone.   I did, grave fathers,
And will maintain he lives with mine own life,
And that this creature told me. [*Aside.*] I was born
With all good stars my enemies!

  Mosca.   Most grave fathers,
If such an insolence as this must pass   75
Upon me, I am silent; 'twas not this
For which you sent, I hope.

  2nd Avocatore.   Take him away.

  Volpone. [*Aside.*] Mosca!

  3rd Avocatore.   Let him be whipped.

  Volpone.   [*Aside.*] Wilt thou betray me?
Cozen me?

  3rd Avocatore. And taught to bear himself
Toward a person of his rank.

  4th Avocatore. [*The Officers seize Volpone.*] Away.   80

  Mosca. I humbly thank your fatherhoods.

  Volpone.   [*Aside.*] Soft, soft. Whipped?
And lose all that I have? If I confess,
It cannot be much more.

  4th Avocatore. [*To Mosca.*] Sir, are you married?

  Volpone. [*Aside.*] They'll be allied anon; I must be resolute:
The fox shall here uncase.   *He puts off* 85

  Mosca.   Patron!   *his disguise.*

80 HIS *i.e. Mosca's.*
81 SOFT, SOFT "*Easy, easy.*"
84 ANON *soon.*
85 UNCASE *take off disguise.*

Act V Scene xii

    Volpone.   Nay, now
My ruins shall not come alone; your match
I'll hinder sure. My substance shall not glue you,
Nor screw you, into a family.
    Mosca.   Why, patron!
    Volpone. I am Volpone, and this is my knave;
90 This, his own knave; this, avarice's fool;
This, a chimera of wittol, fool, and knave.
And, reverend fathers, since we all can hope
Nought but a sentence, let's not now despair it.
You hear me brief.
    Corvino.   May it please your fatherhoods—
    Commendatore.   Silence.
95   *1st Avocatore.* The knot is now undone by miracle!
    2nd Avocatore. Nothing can be more clear.
    3rd Avocatore.   Or can more prove
These innocent.
    1st Avocatore. Give 'em their liberty.
    Bonario. Heaven could not long let such gross crimes be
hid
    2nd Avocatore. If this be held the highway to get riches,
100 May I be poor!
    3rd Avocatore. This's not the gain, but torment.
    1st Avocatore. These possess wealth as sick men possess fevers,
Which trulier may be said to possess them.
    2nd Avocatore. Disrobe that parasite.

87 SUBSTANCE *fortune.*
89–91 THIS . . . THIS *he points in turn to Mosca, Voltore, Corbaccio, and*
    Corvino.
89 KNAVE *servant.*
91 CHIMERA *mythical beast, part lion, goat and serpent.*
93 LET'S . . . IT *"don't disappoint us by delay."*
94 BRIEF *(speak) briefly.*

Corvino, Mosca.   Most honored fathers—

1st Avocatore. Can you plead aught to stay the course of justice?
If you can, speak.

Corvino, Voltore. We beg favor.

Celia.   And mercy.   105

1st Avocatore. You hurt your innocence, suing for the guilty.
Stand forth; and first the parasite. You appear
T'have been the chiefest minister, if not plotter,
In all these lewd impostures; and now, lastly,
Have with your impudence abused the court,   110
And habit of a gentleman of Venice,
Being a fellow of no birth or blood.
For which our sentence is, first thou be whipped;
Then live perpetual prisoner in our galleys.

Volpone. I thank you for him.

Mosca.   Bane to thy wolfish nature.   115

1st Avocatore. Deliver him to the *Saffi.* [*Mosca is taken out.*]
    Thou Volpone,
By blood and rank a gentleman, canst not fall
Under like censure; but our judgment on thee
Is that thy substance all be straight confiscate
To the hospital of the *Incurabili.*   120
And since the most was gotten by imposture,
By feigning lame, gout, palsy, and such diseases
Thou art to lie in prison, cramped with irons,
Till thou be'st sick and lame indeed. Remove him.

Volpone. This is called mortifying of a fox.   125

108 MINISTER *agent.*
109 LEWD IMPOSTURES *base pretenses.*
115 BANE TO *a curse on.*
116 SAFFI *bailiffs.*
119 STRAIGHT CONFISCATE *instantly confiscated.*
120 INCURABILI *incurables.*
125 MORTIFYING *N.*

    1st Avocatore. Thou, Voltore, to take away the scandal
Thou hast giv'n all worthy men of thy profession,
Art banished from their fellowship, and our state.
Corbaccio, bring him near! We here possess
130 Thy son of all thy state, and confine thee
To the monastery of *San' Spirito*;
Where, since thou knew'st not how to live well here,
Thou shalt be learned to die well.
    Corbaccio. [*Cupping his ear.*]   Ha! What said he?
    Commendatore. You shall know anon, sir.
    1st Avocatore.   Thou, Corvino, shalt
135 Be straight embarked from thine own house, and rowed
Round about Venice, through the Grand Canal,
Wearing a cap with fair long ass's ears
Instead of horns; and so to mount, a paper
Pinned on thy breast, to the *Berlina*—
    Corvino.   Yes,
140 And have mine eyes beat out with stinking fish,
Bruised fruit, and rotten eggs—'Tis well, I'm glad
I shall not see my shame yet.
    1st Avocatore.   And to expiate
Thy wrongs done to thy wife, thou art to send her
Home to her father, with her dowry trebled.
145 And these are all your judgments.
    All.   Honored fathers!
    1st Avocatore. Which may not be revoked. Now you begin,
When crimes are done and past, and to be punished,

130 STATE *property*.
131 SAN' SPIRITO *N.*
133 LEARNED *taught.*
135 EMBARKED *put on a boat.*
139 BERLINA *the stage on which malefactors were exposed, the pillory.*
140 EYES BEAT OUT *the crowd threw refuse at those in pillory.*
143–4 *N.*

To think what your crimes are. Away with them!
Let all that see these vices thus rewarded,
Take heart, and love to study 'em. Mischiefs feed   150
Like beasts, till they be fat, and then they bleed.   [*Exeunt.*]
      [*Volpone comes forward.*]
   Volpone. The seasoning of a play is the applause.
Now, though the fox be punished by the laws,
He yet doth hope there is no suff'ring due
For any fact which he hath done 'gainst you.   155
If there be, censure him; here he doubtful stands.
If not, fare jovially, and clap your hands.

155 FACT *crime.*

THE END

Notes

DEDICATION

PRESENTATION *At some time after* Volpone *had been played in London by the King's Men (Shakespeare's company) in the winter of 1605–06, the play was presented at Oxford and Cambridge. The probable date of these performances is the summer of 1606.*

EPISTLE

34–6 *Blasphemy, obscenity, and lack of moral purpose were the standard charges leveled by the Puritans in their continuing war against the theaters. By 1606 there was some substance to their accusations, as Jonson admits, for in the sensational plays of some writers like John Marston and Thomas Middleton there is a pronounced tendency to seek out the obscene for its own sake. The best description of this new sensationalism in the theater is to be found in* Alfred Harbage, Shakespeare and the Rival Tradition, *New York, 1952. Jonson in the Induction to* Every Man out of His Humor *describes more fully the poetic practices to which he objects.*

48 WITH ALL HIS TEETH *Richard III was popularly believed to have been born with a full set of teeth, and Shakespeare, following tradition, makes of this a fearful omen of Richard's later unnatural behavior. See* Rich. III, II.4.

52 ALLOWED *Licensed for public production by the Master of the Revels, a court official who acted as censor in Elizabethan times. This power later passed to the Lord Chamberlain, who, through a deputy called the censor, still exercises it.*

52 THOSE . . . MINE *Jonson was the part author of a number of plays, among them* Eastward Ho *(1604), which he wrote with Chapman and Marston. This play, though it was produced, was definitely not allowed, and Jonson went*

to jail, along with Chapman and Marston, for certain passages in it which offended King James.

75 FOOLS AND DEVILS *The reference here is to the old-fashioned morality plays and early Elizabethan drama modeled on these, in which fools of the slapstick variety, clowning devils, and melodramatic Vices were stocks in trade. The playwrights of the early 17th century, and Jonson particularly, were extremely self-conscious of writing a more sophisticated type of play, and they looked back with tolerant scorn on earlier plays, "antique relics of barbarism," and even on such recent drama of the ranting variety as Kyd's* The Spanish Tragedy *and Marlowe's* Tamburlaine. *For an example of Jonson's amused treatment of devils and the older type play see the opening scene of* The Devil Is an Ass.

81-2 THE WRITER *The sense of this entire passage is somewhat difficult because Jonson leaps from subject to subject. Here it is necessary to realize that "the writer" and the man who considers that some foolish character in a play is a caricature of himself are one and the same. Jonson has in mind the so-called "War of the Theaters" in which he is supposed to have caricatured John Marston and Thomas Dekker. These writers took their revenge by putting Jonson in a play. The alternating process went on for several years. Jonson is here objecting that he never really meant to satirize any particular person, and arguing, in the age-old manner of satirists, that by being angry, the victim identifies himself with the fool in the play.*

91 A NAME Horace. *Thomas Dekker in his play* Satiromastix (1601) *presented Jonson, in a ridiculous manner, under the name of Horace. Jonson had previously used Horace as the satirist in his* Poetaster.

105 AS . . . PROMISE *According to the critics, comedy was supposed to end joyfully. This "comic law" was purportedly derived from the practice of classical comedy, but as Jonson points out a few lines later on, not all the plays of Aristophanes, Plautus, and Terence end on a happy note.*

110 WE . . . INTERLUDES *Another common Puritan complaint against the theater.*

116-17 TO . . . SPEAK *Jonson probably refers to his commentary on Horace's* Ars Poetica, *on which he had announced a year or two before that he was working. The commentary does not survive, and it seems likely that it was lost when Jonson's library burned several years later.*

133 CINNAMUS THE BARBER *In Elizabethan days the barber often was a surgeon as well and would be called on to remove such marks as Jonson, figuratively, plans to make on the poetasters who have whored the Muse. Martial*

in one of his epigrams (6.64.26) mentions the skill of Cinnamus in removing "stigmata."

137 BLACKFRIARS *A fashionable residential area in the heart of the City of London. Several indoor theaters were in this area.*

PERSONS OF THE PLAY

VOLPONE *At the basis of this play is a beast fable—much like those told by Aesop and retold with variations during the Middle Ages—in which the fox, pretending to be dying, attracts the birds of prey only to outwit them in the end. The names of the chief characters are forms of animal names: Volpone, the fox; Mosca, the fly; Voltore, the vulture; Corbaccio and Corvino, ravens; Sir Pol, the Parrot; and Peregrine, a hunting hawk.*

VENICE *In Jonson's time Venice was known not only for its connection with trade but also for its wealth, luxury, sophistication, and political cunning. The first act of* Othello *provides an excellent picture of what Venice meant to the Renaissance Englishman.*

PROLOGUE

12 "HE WAS A YEAR ABOUT THEM" *It was one of Jonson's boasts that he was a craftsman who worked and reworked his plays rather than turning them out hurriedly, as most Elizabethan playwrights apparently did. In the satirical treatment of Jonson as Horace in* Satiromastix *this boast is ridiculed (V.2.202).*

17–18 COADJUTOR . . . TUTOR *Elizabethan playing companies were repertory companies requiring vast numbers of plays. Plays were thus usually treated as mere commodities and were often written by factory methods. The various forms which this method could take are referred to in this list:* coadjutor, *a co-writer who wrote part of a play, as Jonson wrote part of* Eastward Ho; novice, *an apprentice doing parts under a master's direction—Richard Brome, later a dramatist in his own right, was Jonson's novice;* journeyman, *a specialist called in to repair plays and rewrite parts, as Jonson wrote additions to* The Spanish Tragedy; tutor, *a guide and corrector of what others wrote—in later life Jonson, whose reputation was by then assured, often performed this function for other poets and playwrights.*

In this passage, and throughout the Epistle and the Prologue, Jonson is anxious to make it clear that he is a poet with the loftiest understanding of his art and not a mere writer of plays seeking to make a living by pleasing his audience. No doubt the length of Jonson's explanations was necessitated by the fact that the Elizabethans denied the elevated name of poet to mere playwrights, and that Jonson, from the time he began working in the theater, about 1598–99, had been engaged in all the activities he now scorns. At one time he was an actor and early in his career he worked as a play-patcher for the theatrical entrepreneur Philip Henslowe. He had undoubtedly engaged in personal quarrels with other playwrights, caricaturing them in his plays, and these satiric activities had recently been exposed in Dekker's Satiromastix.

21 QUAKING CUSTARDS The usual explanation of this term is that it refers to a huge custard brought in at city feasts and made the source of many foolish tricks. But it is difficult to see how a custard can be "with fierce teeth affrighted." John Marston writes, "Let custards quake, my rage must freely run," in his satirical poem The Scourge of Villainy (1598–99), and the word "Custards" refers to the bumbling fools whom he is prepared to attack in his fierce satiric style (Satire II, line 4). Jonson in his Poetaster, where he objects to the outlandish style of the verse satirists, makes Crispinus (Marston) the false poet vomit up this term along with a number of others (V.3.525). In 1599, when the further printing of verse satire was forbidden, Marston carried his satiric style to the theater, where for a number of years his dramatic satirists proceeded with "fierce teeth" to frighten "quaking custards." It is, I believe, such satiric plays as Marston's Histriomastix and The Malcontent that Jonson is referring to here.

27 STOL'N FROM EACH TABLE The comparison is to scraps stolen from a feast. The Elizabethan playwright was notorious for lifting material from the classics and from his contemporaries. Since no playwright borrowed from the classics more readily than Jonson—the present play is a tissue of lines and situations borrowed from every comic writer from Aristophanes to Erasmus— he must have in mind some distinction between the writer who simply lifts whole passages and the writer like himself, who reworks and recombines the old material into a new play.

31 LAWS . . . PERSONS During the 16th century a number of critics had set up from Aristotle's Poetics several laws supposed to govern dramatic representation. The law of time limited stage time to twenty-four hours; the law of place limited stage action to an area which could be realistically traveled in the space of time allowed; and the law of persons limited growth and change in characters to an amount that could realistically occur in twenty-four hours. Obviously the average Elizabethan playwright payed no attention to these "laws," but Jonson adhered to them rather closely. His qualification in line 32, "needful rule," suggests his basic attitude toward the "laws."

Act I, Scene i

1 [VOLPONE] *Jonson does not provide a speech ascription for the first speech in a scene but simply lists the characters present at the beginning of the scene. In this edition the lists of characters are deleted and the necessary speech ascription added, without further comment.*

5 PEEP . . . RAM *The Ram is the sign of Aries in the zodiac. The sun enters Aries on the 21st of March, the spring equinox, and from this time the "teeming" earth can look forward to increasing light, warmth, and growth.*

15 THAT AGE *A number of classical poets, Ovid particularly (see* Metamorphoses *1.89–112), looked back to a mythical golden age when men lived simpler and more honest lives, and which, according to the myth, was distinguished by its lack of precious metals. The discovery of gold and jewels always brings about the transition from the age of gold to the ages of bronze, silver, and, at last, iron. Volpone completely misunderstands the metaphorical meaning of "gold" in the traditional term.*

40 USURE *Volpone refers here to the practice of men loaning money at exorbitant rates to individuals in need, particularly to young men of fashion living beyond their means, the "soft prodigals" of line 41. This entire passage through line 66 is a catalogue of the various means by which the growing Elizabethan mercantile class made their fortunes. Although Volpone disdains these "common" ways of making money, Jonson is not setting all these business practices up as honest ways of life. Many of them are the comparatively new methods of the entrepreneur who, in contrast to the medieval craftsmen, made money by risking money rather than by making a product and then selling it. For a full description of the new economic practices Jonson refers to here and the older medieval practices which are being silently invoked as a standard, see L. C. Knights,* Drama and Society in the Age of Jonson, *London, 1937.*

76 CLIENTS *Although Volpone uses the word in the general sense of "dependents," the word also looks back to the original Latin meaning: free men who, lacking Roman citizenship, placed themselves under the protection of a wealthy Roman who then became their "patron." Ideally the situation was one of mutual dependence and support, but under the Empire the arrangement degenerated into a nominal relationship between wealthy vanity on one side and servile, flattering poverty on the other. By use of the word "clients"— and Mosca's frequent use of the word "patron"—Jonson evokes another image of social degeneration.*

Act I, Scene ii

1 *The entertainment put on by Nano and Androgyno provides a good example of the complexity and range of Jonson's dramatic technique. Most immediately what we have here is a scene of sophisticated degeneracy: a dwarf and a hermaphrodite act out a dialogue in which such matters as souls, religion, war, and philosophy are treated in a mocking, cynical fashion. The scorn of these cynics for such matters is driven home by the use of the old-fashioned, stumbling, four-stress meter—the implication being that only in the crude, old-fashioned plays which employed this verse form were such matters as the soul taken seriously. Mosca, the author of the entertainment, derived much of this mock-history of the soul from another cynical and sophisticated author, the 2nd-century Greek satirist Lucian, in whose* Dream or Dialogue of the Cobbler and the Cock *a cock tells his owner, a poor cobbler, of the various transmigrations of soul which have brought him at last to the barnyard. But this tale of Lucian's has a point to which Mosca does not refer: the cobbler is eaten up with envy of a friend of his who has become wealthy, and the cock in the end succeeds in showing the cobbler what miserable lives the wealthy lead. The moral of the story thus has an immediate bearing on the events of the play and reflects back in an ironic fashion on the gold-worshiping household of Volpone. These clever people are condemning themselves from their own mouths.*

The scene has, however, a third dimension. It is a brief announcement of the central theme of the play. We have here a short and irreverent history of the progressive degeneration of mankind—the soul which comes first from Apollo, ends at last in a fool and a hermaphrodite—and in the body of the play itself the characters pass through a variety of assumed shapes, ending in the forms of ridicule and sickness which the court forces them into at the end of the play. Volpone, for example, while imagining himself actually to be in his cleverness the "paragon of animals," passes successively through the shapes of a sick man, a mountebank, an "impotent," and finally an inmate of a prison for incurables. Harry Levin, "Jonson's Metempsychosis," PQ 22, 1943, compares this scene to other contemporary treatments of the theme of degeneration, such as Donne's Anniversaries.

2 PLAY . . . SHOW *Nano is pointing out—in mockingly humble tones—that his entertainment is a small affair and not to be judged by the standards applicable to a play put on in the public playhouses or to one of the learned productions of the students at the universities, where classical plays or strict*

imitations of the dramas of Seneca, Terence, and Plautus were often performed.

8 FAST AND LOOSE *A gambling trick, somewhat like our "shell game," in which a leather belt was folded cleverly a number of times, and a dagger driven in between the folds. Bets were then made on whether the belt was fast or loose, i.e. around the dagger or free of it.*

26 "BY QUATER" *Pythagoras believed that number was the principle of harmony in the universe, and he therefore attached supernatural significance to the geometrical relationships. The "quater" referred to here is the triangle made with four as its base:*

```
        •

      •   •

    •   •   •

  •   •   •   •
```

75 FREE FROM SLAUGHTER *The rhyme "laughter-slaughter" is a somewhat unusual one, and shortly after* Volpone *was played, John Marston, who had long engaged in satirical exchanges with Jonson (see above, N. to Epistle), commented in his play* The Fawne *on the foolish critic who "vowed to get the consumption of the lungs, or to leave to posterity the true pronunciation and orthography of laughing" (IV.1). For a discussion of the various possibilities of rhyming these words see Helge Kökeritz,* Shakespeare's Pronunciation *(New Haven, 1953), pp. 183-4.*

123 'TIS . . . NOW *Throughout the remainder of this scene Volpone remains in bed. The bed might have been placed in a small curtained space at the rear of the platform stage, but since most of the action takes place around the bed it would seem more likely that it was placed somewhere toward the front, where the facial expression of the "sick man" could have been seen and his low, faltering words heard. To meet this dramatic problem a bed could have been set up on the stage proper or within a small tent, or "mansion," placed forward of the tiring-house wall. For a description of these mansions and a discussion of their use see C. Walter Hodges,* The Globe Restored *(New York, 1954), pp. 58-61. See also A. M. Nagler,* Shakespeare's Stage, *New Haven, 1958.*

124-7 NOW . . . HOPES *These four lines constitute a mock invocation. Where the poet or petitioner usually calls on the gods for inspiration, Volpone, abusing poetry as he abuses other institutions of mankind, calls on sickness. For another example of Volpone's sacrilegious poetry see the mock aubade —song to the dawn—with which the play begins.*

Act I, Scene iv

46 FROM HIS BRAIN *Drainage of fluid from the brain was believed to be one of the final stages of the disease, strong apoplexy, which Mosca is describing so carefully, symptom by symptom. Corbaccio's excited interruption at this point shows that he is fully aware of the significance of this symptom, and that he now believes his dearest hope is about to be realized.*

73 POTABILE *Medicine having gold as its principal ingredient was believed to be a sovereign remedy for all diseases, and it is this compound which Mosca and Corbaccio discuss in the following lines.*

128 MY BROTHER *There is a glancing but significant reference here to the biblical story (Genesis 27) in which Jacob defrauds his brother Esau of Isaac's blessing by disguising himself in the skin of a goat.*

156 AESON *The father of Jason, captain of the Argonauts, who was restored to youth by the black magic of Medea.*

Act I, Scene v

100-3 *The English were much laughed at abroad for the freedom with which they allowed their ladies to come and go as they pleased and without supervision.*

126 HE *On entering and leaving his house Corvino questions his guards on each particular of their instructions. He has, the passage suggests, turned his house into a fortress to guard his wife.*

129 MAINTAIN . . . SHAPE *In a play in which changing shape—i.e. appearance—is a leading theme, this line is thoroughly ambiguous; but Volpone's surface meaning is that he agrees with Mosca that he must wear a disguise when he goes out, for if the bilking of the fools is to succeed he must always be thought of as a dying man.*

Act II, Scene i

10 ULYSSES *Ulysses is described in the opening lines of* The Odyssey *as a man who "roamed the wide world and saw the cities of many peoples and learned their ways." He became for the Renaissance the prototype of the curious traveler and a model for the young men of fashion who completed their education with a journey abroad. Their purpose was, of course, to know "men's minds and manners," and Sir Politic reveals his own lack of sense in his scorn for this project.*

17 MY LORD AMBASSADOR *Sir Henry Wotton, King James' ambassador at Venice, was himself a noted intriguer.*

34 LION'S WHELPING IN THE TOWER *A lioness, Elizabeth, was at this time kept in the Tower of London, and she produced cubs in 1604 and again in 1605.*

36–7 FIRES . . . STAR *In 1604 there were reports of ghostly armies fighting at Berwick, on the Scottish border, and Kepler discovered a new star in the constellation Serpentarius. Mass hallucinations were very common in England during this period, and there were many reports of battles in the clouds and other ominous sights.*

38 METEORS *Meteors, because they are a disruption of the ordinary pattern of the heavens, were taken as ominous portents of impending social disorder.*

46 WHALE *A whale did come up the Thames at this time, within eight miles of London, and the fearful believed that it intended to pump all the water from the river onto the land.*

51 SPINOLA *The Spanish general in the Netherlands at this time. He was extremely successful amd was believed by the gullible in England to be fantastically clever in devising cunning schemes and "secret weapons."*

53 STONE *A well-known London clown who had been flogged not long before* Volpone *was written for making mocking speeches about the Lord Admiral.*

80 TOOTHPICK *All of Sir Politic's descriptions of plots, spies, and methods of espionage are burlesques not of genuine activities but of those imagined by the foolish and timorous in the days immediately after the discovery of the Gunpowder Plot, a Catholic attempt to blow up King James and the assembled Parliament on November 4, 1605.*

90 MAMALUCHI *Plural form of "Mameluke," former Christian slaves of the Turks who became rulers of Egypt during the 13th century. Sir Pol is simply seizing on any rare word to support his pretense of knowing all about every matter of state.*

Act II, Scene ii

SD *There is no longer any exact equivalent of the mountebank and his show, but the old-fashioned Indian Medicine Man with his traveling wagon, his show, his "snake oil," and his "spiel" was in the direct line of descent from the mountebank. A picture of the type of stage referred to here is reproduced in P. L. Duchartre,* The Italian Comedy *(1929), p. 63, where the crowd,* including one figure called "Inglese," is gathered around stages set up in St. Mark's Square. The date of this print is 1610.

2 BANK Sir Pol is apparently correct, for the accepted etymology of "mountebank" is the Italian monta in banco. Bench (Italian, banco) here means the basic platform stage—simply boards laid on trestles with perhaps a cloth backdrop. George Kernodle's recent theory about this type of stage seems to fit the situation in Volpone. Kernodle first argued that the physical details of the Elizabethan theater served as symbols of the social and cosmic order and therefore the action in the plays always took place before concrete reminders of a solid, unchanging reality. But, he continues: "The true historical prototype of the modern open stage is . . . the mounte-bank theater that dates from the Middle Ages. That stage was free and empty, uncluttered by symbols of social or cosmic order for the simple reason that the medieval mountebank, peddling his snake oil and entertaining on the streets, was the first completely isolated individual. He had no place in medieval society. He was an outcast, a vagabond. Everyone else had a place—a set place—and all other stages of the time had elaborate scenic symbols of the temporal order." "The Open Stage: Elizabethan or Existentialist?" Shakespeare Survey, 12 (1960), p. 3. The term "isolated individual" describes Volpone perfectly, and his actions throughout the play are those of a man who considers himself entirely free of the normal controls imposed by society or nature. It should be noted, however, that Volpone's mountebank stage is a theater erected within a theater—a play within a play—and that although he is unaware of the irony of his situation, the stable order still stands unchanged in the details of the larger theater and mocks his pretensions to absolute freedom.

22 SCOTO OF MANTUA A 16th-century Italian actor and leader of a troupe of players licensed by the Duke of Mantua. Scoto was a renowned juggler and sleight-of-hand artist who appeared in England about 1576 and performed before the Queen and her court. By the time Volpone was written Scoto's name had become, in England, synonymous with the skillful deceiver.

36 PROCURATIA Here and in the remainder of Scoto's speech the geographical details are quite correct, and the biographical details, though no source is known for them, form a plausible enough description of the life of a traveling actor and mountebank in 16th-century Italy. But certain details, both geographical and biographical, suggest that under the cover of 16th-century Venice, Jonson is talking about early 17th-century London and his own life as a playwright.

At least, the fortunes and character of Scoto and Ben Jonson are sufficiently similar to be worthy of note. *Scoto is now playing in an "obscure nook" after having usually played in "face of the public Piazza"; Jonson was now presenting* Volpone *at the Globe Theatre, on the south bank of the Thames, after several years in which his plays, with one exception,* Sejanus, *had been acted at Blackfriars, a private theater in the center of the city.* Scoto refers to false reports that he had been sent to the galleys recently for insulting Cardinal Bembo; *Jonson had actually been imprisoned in 1605 for his part in a play,* Eastward Ho, *which contained passages offensive to King James. Scoto has only scorn for the common mountebanks,* ground ciarlitani, who take their stories from collections like Boccaccio's Decameron and perform only for the delight of their vulgar audience, "your shriveled, salad-eating artisans"; Jonson had from the beginning of his dramatic career been contemptuous of the petty playwrights of the day who borrowed liberally from other authors to provide sensational theatrical fare for the groundlings, while he, like *Scoto, had followed the "craggy paths of study" to arrive at the "flowery plains of honor and reputation."* Sixpence is the final price of Scoto's elixir, and it may well have been the price of admission to the earliest performances of Volpone. The Globe Theatre, where the play was first performed, was a public theater, where the standard admission fee was a penny, with additional payments up to twopence for better seats. Herford and Simpson (9, 196) note, however, a passage from Jasper Mayne, Jonsonus Virbius (1638) lines 67–8:

> So when thy FOXE had ten times acted beene,
> Each day was first, but that 'twas cheaper seene.

They consider this a reference to the "higher prices of earliest performances"; *and if I am correct about the parallel between Scoto of Mantua and Ben Jonson of London, it seems likely that sixpence was the price of general admission to the first performances of* Volpone.

Scoto-Volpone is, of course, a charlatan, the nostrum he sells worthless, and the language he uses mere spiel; but Jonson is, I believe, working here *in an ironic fashion, as he does so regularly in this play.* Just as Volpone's opening speech on gold calls our attention to those vital natural and social forces which have been perverted by the substitution of a gold coin for the sun, *so here our attention is focused on the nature of true medicine,* and true *playing, by the distortion of both those arts wrought by greed and lust, the moving powers behind Scoto-Volpone's performance. But Jonson's nostrum, his satiric plays, are, the speech implies, the true moral medicine for a sick* world, and they represent the standard of playwrighting against which Scoto's false play is measured.

46 BEMBO'S *Cardinal Bembo (1470–1547) was a famous Italian humanist noted for his pure Latin style and for the beautiful culminating speech he delivers in Castiglione's* Il Cortegiano *(1528) on the progress from love of earthly beauty to love of the spiritual. Castiglione's book was translated into English as* The Book of the Courtier *by Sir Thomas Hoby in 1561 and became a handbook for the Renaissance English gentleman.*

51–2 BOCCACCIO . . . FABULIST *Giovanni Boccaccio (1313?–75) whose collection of tales (fables)* The Decameron *was a storehouse for later storytellers.*

90 FLUX, OR CATARRH *Volpone's medicine throughout this speech is based on the medieval and Renaissance theory of the four humors and the four elements, which eventually goes back to Aristotelian physics. The four elements and their qualities were: earth (cold, heavy, and dry), water (cold, heavy, and wet), air (warm, light, and wet), and fire (hot, light, and dry). These four elements were the building blocks out of which everything, including physical man, was believed to be constructed. In man the elements took the form of humors or fluids, the four cardinal humors being blood, phlegm, choler, and melancholy or black choler. In the healthy man the humors were, theoretically, balanced, but in the majority of men one humor predominated and determined a man's "humor" or temperament: sanguine, phlegmatic, choleric, melancholic. When the humors became seriously unbalanced, sickness resulted, and the "humid flux" Volpone refers to is an excess of heavy wetness flowing out of the head into the body—we should probably call it arthritis. In his earlier humor plays,* Every Man In His Humor *and* Every Man Out of His Humor, *Jonson had translated the concept of humors from the physical to the psychic realm and had defined a humor as a situation in which,*

> *some one particular quality*
> *Doth so possess a man, that it doth draw*
> *All his affects, his spirits, and his powers,*
> *In their confluctions, all to run one way . . .*
> ("*After the Second Sounding,*" *lines 105–8.*)

101 MAL CADUCO *epilepsy,* TREMOR CORDIA *palpitation of the heart,* RETIRED NERVES *shrunken sinews,* THE STONE *kidney stone,* STRANGURY *difficult urination,* HERNIA VENTOSA *tumor containing gas,* ILIACA PASSIO *cramps of the small intestine.*

118 BROUGHTON'S BOOKS *Hugh Broughton (1549–1617) was a Puritan minister and scholar who wrote a number of strange books on religious subjects. Jonson's intense dislike of the Puritans regularly finds expression in his plays.*

129 GONSWART *Identity not known certainly, but perhaps the theologian Johannes Wessel of Gansfort (1420–89).*

130 PARACELSUS . . . LONG SWORD *Paracelsus was one of the strangest and most noted of the early Renaissance physician-magicians. Alchemy and physic were for him but part of one subject. He was supposed to have kept his secret "essences" in the handle of his sword.*

SD CELIA AT WINDOW *Celia is on the upper stage above and at the rear of the Elizabethan stage, or at a windowed projection to the side of this balcony.*

244 VIRGINAL JACKS *The virginal was a small spinet without legs, and its "jack" was a board with quills which plucked the strings as the keys were played. But the reference here is probably to the keys, which resemble teeth.*

Act II, Scene iii

2 SCENE *Renaissance critical theory prescribed as the proper setting or "scene" for comedy a public place backing on private houses. Although the literal meaning applies well enough here, the larger meaning of "scene" as "setting for a play" should not be overlooked, for Volpone has just acted out a play of his own devising.*

3–8 FLAMINIO . . . FRANCISCINA . . . PANTALONE *These are all names connected with the commedia dell' arte, the popular Italian street comedy of the 16th and 17th centuries. The plays, put on by traveling troupes playing on stages like those used by Scoto, were improvisations in which each actor played a stock role and put his part together out of memorized lines, speeches, and stage actions called lazzi. The plot was also improvised as the play proceeded. There have been references to the commedia throughout the mountebank's speech—"Zany," "Tabarin," "Zan Fritada"—and the names which Corvino rolls off show that he recognizes the similarity of the scene here with one of the stock comic situations. Flaminio was a noted actor in the commedia, Franciscina was a standard name for the amorous and witty servant girl, and Pantalone was the name for the old Venetian merchant who is inevitably cuckolded.*

In the mountebank scene Jonson has combined three separate but related forms of showmanship designed to gull the fools: the mountebank crying his wares, the alchemist promising the elixir which will prolong life and beauty, and the street comedian.

Act II, Scene v

11–15 COPPER RINGS . . . STARCHED BEARD *The mountebank then, like all pitchmen still, wore elaborate costumes and make-up to attract his audience. Many believed that the toad had a jewel,* TOAD STONE, *between his eyes which had magical properties. The exact meaning of* COPE-STITCH *is uncertain but doubtless it was a fancy, large stitch of some type which stood out on the ornate embroidered suit. The hearse was traditionally a framework over a tomb used to support rich hangings,* HEARSE CLOTHS. *The implication here is probably that the mountebank has stolen, or at least bought second-hand, these funeral draperies for his clothes. The* TILT FEATHER *was a large, ornate feather or plume worn in helmets; and a* STARCHED BEARD *was one of the extreme fashions of the time.*

24 SAVE . . . DOWRY *By law if a husband could show that his wife had been unfaithful, he gained possession of her dowry, which otherwise remained in the wife's control during her lifetime.*

55–6 CONJURER . . . LAID *The conjurer (magician) who desired to raise a devil drew a magic circle within which he was safe until the devil was returned to hell, i.e. "laid."*

Act III, Scene i

10 SCIENCE *A term formerly applied to certain philosophical studies required for a degree in the School of* Literae Humaniores, *the Liberal Arts—see "liberally professed" in line 11. Mosca is lamenting that the art of the flatterer should be considered only a "mystery," i.e. a mechanical skill or trade, and he is proposing that in view of its prevalence it be raised to the dignity of a science and made, like logic, a required study for all educated men.*

19 GROIN *Mosca implies that pandering, or perhaps, considering the word "receipts," retailing new varieties of sensual pleasure, is among the activities of the "unattached" parasite who out of the poverty of his imagination and his desperate condition is forced to these unworthy tricks—unworthy of the master parasite like Mosca.*

22 LICK . . . MOTH *Mosca is carrying to the extreme that form of servility, common in all ages, in which the flatterer picks threads or other objects from the coats of those he is trying to please. "Moth" had until the 18th century the general meaning of "vermin."*

Act III, Scene iv

47 GOLDEN MEDIOCRITY *Herford and Simpson (9, 715) refer to this phrase as "high sounding nonsense" which Lady Wouldbe invents on the spur of the moment. This is true, but the phrase operates—like most of the apparent nonsense spoken by Jonson's characters—to remind us of ideals being violated and to define the moral status of the characters and action. Here the ideal referred to is the "golden mean," that classic guide to conduct which dictates "nothing in excess," and which has been lost completely in Volpone's world where men pursue gold and power and lust to the exclusion of all else, becoming in the process "golden mediocrities."*

80–1 ARETINE? CIECO DI HADRIA? *The other names Lady Wouldbe reels off are major Italian poets, but Luigi Groto, known as Cieco di Hadria, is a distinctly minor writer, while Pietro Aretino was a writer of powerful but extremely scurrilous and obscene verses. By joining these names to those of the poets of the great tradition Lady Wouldbe betrays her lack of discrimination, her inability to distinguish in literature as in life the profound from the vulgar.*

93–4 PETRARCH ... MUCH *Petrarch was most famous for his love sonnets, which were imitated by generations of poets—Sidney's* Astrophel and Stella *and Spenser's* Amoretti *were in this tradition—and this extensive imitation and borrowing are perhaps the basis for the statement "trusted 'em with much."*

109 OUTWARD THINGS *Lady Wouldbe's psychology is as crude, jargon-ridden, and jumbled as her medicine and her literary criticism, but it does describe roughly what has happened to the characters of the play and the city of Venice—she is using the commonplace Renaissance comparison of man the microcosm and the state or body politic. Man and state in* Volpone *have chosen gold as their idée fixe, and the result has been clouded understanding.*

Act III, Scene v

36 PRIMERO *A popular card game of the day. Volpone makes use of the technical terms of the game—"go less" (i.e. wager less), "draw" and "encounter"—as metaphors for his coming meeting with Celia.*

Act III, Scene vii

119 CROCODILE ... TEARS *The crocodile was proverbially believed to shed tears in order to lure his victims.*

153 BLUE PROTEUS . . . HORNED FLOOD *Proteus was the "old man of the sea" who could change himself at will into any shape—see Odyssey 4.456 ff., where Menelaus struggles with him in many forms.* Blue is a translation of the Latin adjective caerulus, applied to anything connected with the sea. *"Horned flood" refers to the river Achelous—"horned" because it branches and roars—which struggled with Hercules in three forms: bull, serpent, and man-ox.* Volpone, *it should be noticed, here defines his genius as the ability to change shape at will,* and so great is his power, he feels, that he could contend with water itself, the very element of change.

161 GREAT VALOIS Henry of Valois, later Henry III of France, was magnificently entertained in Venice in 1524. Plays were one of the standard features of such entertainments.

162 ANTINOUS Usually identified as the Roman Emperor Hadrian's favorite courtier, noted for his physical beauty.

165 SONG This is an imitation of and partly translated from the famous fifth ode of Catullus beginning, Vivamus, mea Lesbia, atque amemus. *The song is lovely but it evokes here not so much an image of a beautiful love seizing its moment, as of the ultimate faithlessness of Catullus' Clodia, the* Lesbia of the poem, and her degeneration into a sensuality as gross as Volpone's.

194 MAY . . . ST. MARK It may be that some image of St. Mark, the patron saint of Venice, had jewels for eyes, and that the jewel Volpone holds up makes them seem trivial, "puts out," by comparison. But at the same time, the jewel "puts out" or obliterates the eyes of the Saint in the same way that Volpone's gold in the opening scene "darkens" the light of the sun (line 6).

215 PANTHERS' BREATH This is, of course, the supreme touch of rarity in Volpone's catalogue of sensual pleasures, and it topples the speech into the ludicrous. But again the particular detail is meaningful: panthers were popularly believed to have an extraordinarily sweet smell which attracted their prey, like the tears of the crocodile referred to in the note to line 119 above. The images which run through this speech, and through the play, are used unselfconsciously by the speakers, but they serve to identify the characters and their world. Mosca crying for Bonario is the crocodile luring its prey with tears; Volpone tempting Celia with "sensual baits" is the sweet-smelling panther; and the world he moves in is the same world as that of Nero's Rome in which a province could be stripped by a Roman general and all its treasures placed in gaudy and vulgar profusion on a woman, Lollia Paulina. This ironic use of imagery is characteristic of Jonson's dramatic technique.

Act IV, Scene i

2 MENTIONED *In the advice to Peregrine which Sir Politic delivers in the remainder of the scene he details the perfect formula for becoming an arrant fop and fool. Concerned only with the outside of man, he makes morality a matter of policy—"never speak a truth"—somewhat in the manner of Polonius advising his son Laertes on how to conduct himself in Paris; religion a matter of fashion; and places his major educational emphasis on table manners and mad schemes for getting rich.*

24–5 WERE . . . YOU *"You could be quite content if there were no religion, only the law." It should be remembered that* Volpone *was written in a time of fierce religious quarrels between Protestant and Catholic, and Protestant and Protestant; and the old angers had recently flared again in England on the discovery of the Gunpowder Plot. In times of such trouble it was fashionable for some of the more skeptical and the more elegant to reject all churches and put their trust in the state alone. Jonson was at this time a professed Catholic who held to his religion under considerable pressure.*

26 MACHIAVEL . . . BODIN *Two advanced thinkers of the age whose books were as popular among the intellectuals and their imitators as Nietzsche and Freud are today. Niccolò Machiavelli was the author of* The Prince, *a handbook of Realpolitik; and Jean Bodin had argued in his writings for religious toleration on the grounds that it was obviously impossible to achieve religious agreement.*

46 PROJECTS *Sir Politic is an example of the type of man known as a projector, the idea man of his time who proposed schemes—projects—for making money.*

133 DIARY *Jonson is burlesquing the many travelers of his time who kept and published journals in which they noted every trivial detail of their journeys, like that meticulous observer of petty facts, Captain Lemuel Gulliver.*

138 THREE BEANS *According to Theophrastus in "the Superstitious Man," from which Jonson took this detail, gnawed spur leathers or any other commonplace happening was taken by the superstitious as having supernatural meaning. Beans were traditionally believed to have an expiatory value, something like "knocking on wood."*

Act IV, Scene ii

30 HUMBLED *Literally, brought low, i.e. all the way down to his spurs; past commentators have found here a cutting reference to the cheapening of knighthood by King James, who soon after he became King in 1603 created knights indiscriminately for political reasons.*

35 THE COURTIER, IL CORTEGIANO (1528), by Baldassare Castiglione, the most famous of the Renaissance handbooks on the conduct becoming to a gentleman, or gentlewoman. Lady Wouldbe fails, of course, to meet any of the standards of gentility laid down in this book.

48 SPORUS A young man whom Nero fancied. He had him castrated and then married him with full ceremony. Volpone has Castrone in his private zoo.

51 WHITEFRIARS NATION Whitefriars was a "liberty" within the City of London, one of those areas exempted by Royal Charter in times past from the control of the town. In Jonson's day the outcasts and those fleeing the law who had taken refuge here had set up a state of their own, based on disorder, and even adopted an official thieves' language. The anarchic condition of Whitefriars suggests the new Venice being created by greed and foolishness in Volpone.

56–8 NAY . . . LIQUID J. D. Rea suggests in his edition of Volpone, p. 214, that these lines are addressed to Peregrine. Sir Politic, Rea argues, is so obsessed with plots that he readily accepts his wife's explanation—though he has had considerable difficulty understanding it—that Peregrine is a disguised courtesan. "Liquid" would then mean "clearly to be seen," and "case" could mean, as it often does, "a mask." This explanation is interesting, but there is no way of proving it, and the lines may equally well be an ironic farewell to a crying ("liquid") Lady Wouldbe.

Act IV, Scene iii

16 USE Employ, make use of in social matters; but the word has also a sexual meaning, as does "conceive" in line 18, which Peregrine picks up quickly. Lady Wouldbe is as clumsy as her husband in her choice of language.

Act IV, Scene iv

14 MUMMIA The juice that oozes from embalmed human bodies. It was much prized until fairly recent times as an ingredient for certain medicines. This passage is part of the theme of cannibalism which runs through the play: e.g. I.1.36, "or men, to grind 'em into powder," or I.5.92, "Or fat, by eating once a month a man."

Act IV, Scene v

22 FATHERHOODS' This is a correct title of respect to apply to the venerable judges of Venice, but Voltore makes good use of this fact. By his frequent references to the judges as fathers he establishes a prejudice on their part for

the outraged father, Corbaccio; makes them feel the wrongs done Corbaccio the father are done to them, the fathers of the city. Volpone, a splendid rhetorician himself, is properly appreciative of the fine points of Voltore's art and comments particularly on this device, V.2.33–7.

125 LETTERS . . . HORN An elaborate but common play on the cuckold and his horns. The letter is the "V" which Corvino makes with his fingers on his forehead to manifest his horns. But the joke also involves the "hornbook," the Elizabethan Primer from which the schoolboy learned his letters. These books were single printed sheets covered with thin, transparent horn to preserve them. The letters were thus read "thorough the horn." It should be noted that in this scene the animal imagery present throughout the play is greatly intensified. Not only is Corvino reduced to an ox by his own efforts but all the characters are brought down by the language and lies of the fools to the level of "jennet" or "swine, goat, wolf."

Act IV, Scene vi

2–3 CHAMELEON, HYENA Lady Wouldbe is simply hurling insults, but here again is an excellent instance of Jonson's ironic use of imagery. The chameleon was considered a "fraudulent, ravening, and gluttonous beast," and was famed then as now for its ability to change color to suit its circumstances. The hyena was predominantly a symbol of treachery, but it was believed able to imitate the voices of human beings. Thus—like the animals mentioned earlier, the crocodile with its tears and the panther with its sweet smells—the images of hyena and chameleon define the activities of fools and villains in Volpone: they are basically "ravening and gluttonous" beasts who are able to change color like the chameleon and imitate the voices of men like the hyena. The most useful book of the period describing the strange natures of the animals as the Elizabethans and their predecessors understood them is Edward Topsell's The Historie of the Foure-Footed Beastes, London, 1607. Topsell describes one type of hyena, the Mantichora, who seems to resemble the characters of the play most closely: he has a face like a man, a treble row of teeth top and bottom, "His wildnes such as can never be tamed, and his appetite is especially to the flesh of man" (p. 437).

24 GREAT IMPOSTOR This term means no more literally than "pretender," but the "impostor" is a stock character of classical comedy, and it is of considerable interest that Jonson uses the term, and the related word "imposture," so frequently in connection with Volpone (e.g. III.7.268; IV.5.8, 18; IV.5.141; IV.6.24). According to the Tractatus Coislinianus, believed by

some to be written by Aristotle, comedy has three types of characters: the alazon or impostor, the eiron or ironical type (Peregrine, Mosca) and the bomolochos or buffoon. The alazon is discussed in detail by F. M. Cornford, The Origin of Attic Comedy (London, 1914), Chapter 2, as he appears in the old comedy of Aristophanes and, perhaps, in the various dances and fertility rites from which, according to Cornford, literary comedy developed. In both rites and plays the impostors were, Cornford says, "unwelcome intruders," "impudent and absurd pretenders," as are the standard butts of comedy still familiar to us: the pedant, the minor official, the informer, the doctor, the lawyer. They always appeared at feasts or celebrations to which they had contributed nothing and insisted on sharing, but were always driven off by the hero or eiron with curses and blows. The obvious parallels in Volpone to the stock comic scene are V.3, where Mosca, acting for Volpone, drives the various minor impostors from the "feast" of Volpone's fortune; and V.4, where Peregrine drives Sir Politic from Venice and from any pretense of being a wise statesman. But Jonson's irony is double, at least, and the eirons of one scene, Volpone and Mosca, are revealed at the conclusion of the play as impostors on the larger scene of Venice, intruders on the feast of a society to which they contributed nothing. And so they, along with their dupes, are driven out of society by the court. The parallels between Jonson's play and the older forms of comedy are both interesting and critically useful, but it is impossible to say that Jonson was aware of the history of the word "impostor," even though his familiarity with Aristophanes and his enormous knowledge of the classics makes it probable that he was.

Act V, Scene i

17 HEAT . . . TIME *According to Renaissance physiology, food was turned by the liver into the four humors (see above, N.II.2.90) balanced in the blood. This blood then went to the heart where it created "vital heat." Volpone's absolute equation of this heat with life is, however, a measure of his degeneration from the proper state of man, for it was believed that this vital heat existed in man only to nurture the brain and thus contribute to such higher human functions as understanding and will.*

Act V, Scene ii

59 JIG *Jigs were the stock-in-trade of the low comedians in the Elizabethan theater, where performances usually ended with a jig.*

84 CURTAIN *In Scene 3 Jonson has the stage direction "Volpone peeps from behind a traverse." Either he has retreated into an inner stage across which*

a curtain is drawn, or a curtain is placed on a wire across part of the main stage. A "traverse" may be, however, a movable screen of some variety. Whatever the arrangement, the "curtain" is probably the same one used to cover the bed ordinarily, and the effect is once again to create a stage on a stage, a theater within a theater.

93 ROPE AND DAGGER *Carrying these props was probably a standard symbol of extravagant madness on the Elizabethan stage. See* The Spanish Tragedy, *IV.4, where Hieronimo runs mad. Jonson had once played Hieronimo's part. See also* Faerie Queene, *I.9.29, and Skelton's* Magnyfycence, *lines 2312 ff.*

103 GIRDLE . . . CESTUS *Cestus was added by Jonson to the Folio to explain the meaning of the "strange poetical girdle." The reference is to the girdle of Venus, mentioned by Homer in* The Iliad, *into which was woven "love, desire, sweetness, soft parley, gracefulness, persuasion, and all the powers of Venus."*

Act V, Scene iii

11 THREAD SPUN *Lady Wouldbe can never abandon her elaborate and "learned" phrasing. The myth referred to here is that of the Three Fates. The thread of a man's life was spun by Clothos, measured by Lachesis, and then cut by Atropos.*

Act V, Scene v

6-7 FOX . . . HOLE *Fox-in-the-hole was a game played by English boys. They hopped about on one leg and beat one another with gloves and pieces of leather tied on a string.*

Act V, Scene viii

12-14 MORAL EMBLEMS . . . EMPTINESS *In the emblem books popular at this time drawings of various animals were used to symbolize human vices, which were then explained in verses. Volpone has in mind here a picture of a crow dropping a piece of cheese while the fox below laughs at him. The moral would point out that the bird, or man, who opens his mouth too freely loses his prize.*

Act V, Scene x

2 AVOCATORI *The speech ascription here and in line 20 below reads in Quarto and Folio 1, "Avo." The usual practice of editors has been to assign this line to a particular Avocatore. Here and at line 20 it seems equally reasonable to have all the judges speak.*

35 DEVIL . . . HIM *The "possession" referred to by Corvino in V.10.10 above. Technically, possession was the entry into the body by the evil spirit, while "obsession" was an attack by the devil from without.*

Act V, Scene xii

20 DO . . . SIR? *Considering the speed with which Voltore changes at this point, it seems likely that Volpone manages to make Voltore pierce his disguise.*

24–31 *All of these details: swelling, vomiting crooked pins, eyes strangely set, the appearance of something running in the body from place to place, and the expulsion of some strange animal from the mouth were all taken as signs of possession by the devil. Herford and Simpson point out (9, 731–2) that a number of these symptoms had appeared in a recent sensational case of witchcraft and exorcism. John Darrell, a minister, in the late 1590's had remarkable effectiveness as an exorciser; he was thought to have freed from demonic possession some of the most stubborn cases in England. But in 1599 his activities were shown to have been faked—though he never admitted it —and some of his patients swore that he had coached them, The details of the fraud were published by Samuel Harsnett, future archbishop of York, in a book titled* Discovery of the Fraudulent Practices of John Darrell *(1599).*

53 RECOVERED *Volpone uses this word several times to mean "the problem is solved"; but in a play where disguise and obliterating the truth with false-hood appear so consistently, we must take the word in its literal sense as well: covering reality over once more with pretense.*

125 MORTIFYING *The literal meaning here is "humiliation," but two other senses apply. A cooking term: to mortify an animal was to allow it to hang after it had been killed until the meat became tender. But, as in our term "mortification of the flesh," the word also means subjecting the body and the passions to ascetic discipline and rigorous austerities.*

131 SAN' SPIRITO *The Monastery of the Holy Spirit, where Corbaccio, who has heretofore been completely without soul or spirit, will be painfully instructed to forget the things of this world and prepare his soul for the next.*

143–4 *The return of Celia to her father's house is worth comment. It is usual in comedy for the young lovers to be united in some fashion, often quite an unrealistic one, by the end of the play; and thus the marriage or feast—or even seduction—with which comedy usually ends signals the triumph of vitality, beauty, and cleverness over foolishness and those idiocies which obstruct life rather than furthering it. So general is this pattern in comedy that we anticipate, I believe, in* Volpone *that a way will be found to void the marriage of Corvino and Celia and bring about her union with Bonario. Her return to her single state—celibacy is never a matter for celebration in comedy—is therefore a disruption of the normal comic pattern and a grim reminder that in the world Jonson has here constructed greed and foolishness are not always completely overcome. Even though they may destroy themselves in the end, they nevertheless leave permanent scars on the world.*

Appendix : Text and Sources

Volpone was written in five weeks' time, probably during the winter of 1605–06, and the play was produced by The King's Men, Shakespeare's company, during the early winter of 1606. 1605 is the date given for its first performance on its title page in the folio edition of 1616, but in the Elizabéthan court and legal calendar this could mean anytime before the first of March 1606. Herford and Simpson point out (*9*, 196) that the incident of the whale coming up the Thames referred to by Sir Politic (II.1.47) is perhaps a reference to an event that occurred in late January 1606. The performances at Oxford and Cambridge referred to by Jonson in his dedication took place in either 1606 or 1607.

The play was first published in quarto in 1607 and appeared next in the first volume of Jonson's *Works*, which was printed in 1616. Unlike the majority of the dramatists of his age, Jonson was extremely careful about the publication of his plays, and so both Quarto and Folio give us excellent texts. He corrected the proofs of the Folio, but the changes he made in *Volpone* are relatively minor, chiefly involving spelling and punctuation. The Folio text is the basis of this edition, and where there are variants between it and the quarto which involve meaning or throw some light on a difficult reading, they are recorded in the notes.

The accepted practice in the Elizabethan theater was for the playwright to take a story or plot from another work—history, romance, or older play—and then elaborate on this basic structure. In nearly every one of Shakespeare's thirty-seven plays, for example, we know that he drew his plot from a particular source. But Jonson usually worked in a different manner, and despite a number of attempts to show that one particular work or another was the source of *Volpone*, it is by now clear that his plot, while it has many analogues, is his own work. If Shakespeare began with a story, Jonson began with an idea for which he then proceeded to construct an appropriate action. And since he was a very learned and extremely well-read man for whom literature was a living thing, inevitably his idea focused lines, characters, and situations from his reading, and these are echoed in his play and mingled with contemporary events to create that tone of historical density so characteristic of his works. This effect is discussed in more detail in the introduction at the beginning of the present volume.

The range and number of these echoes are enormous, and it is regrettable that the limitation of space in this edition does not permit each one to be noted and commented upon. Aesop's fables, The Bible, Juvenal, Horace, Aristophanes, Tacitus, Pindar, and many others contribute something, and it thus may be said that *Volpone* has either a great many sources or none at all. Two of these "sources," or parallels as I should prefer to call them, should be mentioned, because they contribute a good deal to the play and because both have been advanced as the true source. J. D. Rea in the preface to his edition argues that Jonson constructed *Volpone* almost entirely from Erasmus' famous satire *The Praise of Folly*. Rea's case is overstated, but the notes to his edition which point out the parallels provide a most useful insight into Jonson's use of other literary works. A number of other scholars have argued that Jonson based his play on the *Satyricon* of Petronius Arbiter, a Latin satire of the first century A.D. Jonson doubtless made use of this work, and he may have taken from sections 116–17 the idea of legacy hunting, *captatus*, which was not the common practice in Renaissance England or Italy that it apparently was in Rome of the first century. This practice was, however, satirized by both Horace and Juvenal in works which are verbally echoed in *Volpone*.

Selected Reading List

EDITIONS

Ben Jonson, ed. C. H. Herford and Percy Simpson, 11 vols., Oxford, 1925–52. The standard edition of Jonson's complete works. Volumes 1 and 2 contain a biography of Jonson and introductions to the plays.

Volpone, ed. J. D. Rea, Yale Studies in English, 59, New Haven, 1919.

CRITICISM

Barish, Jonas, "The Double Plot in *Volpone*," *Modern Philology*, 51 (1954), 172–93.

Eliot, T. S., "Ben Jonson," in *Selected Essays 1917–1932* (New York, 1932), pp. 127–39.

Ellis-Fermor, Una, "Ben Jonson," in *The Jacobean Drama* (London 1936), pp. 98–117.

Enck, J. J., *Jonson and the Comic Truth*, Madison, 1957.

Knights, L. C., *Drama and Society in the Age of Jonson*, London, 1937.
  "Ben Jonson, Dramatist," in *The Age of Shakespeare*, Vol. 2 of the Pelican Guide to English Literature, London, 1955.

Levin, Harry, Introduction to *Ben Jonson, Selected Works*, New York, 1938.

Partridge, Edward, *The Broken Compass*, New York, 1958.